New+
GET UP TO SPEED

New Get Up to Speed + *Situational* helps students learn how to speak like a native speaker by focusing on contemporary language usage in everyday situations supplemented with modern facts and cultural notions.

Key Features
- Warm Up Activity
- Useful Expressions
- Key Conversation
- Language Practice
- Role Plays
- Cultural Discussion Questions
- Slang & Idioms

MP3

CARROT HOUSE

CARROT HOUSE

New Get Up To Speed+ 2 Situational
© Carrot House

All rights reserved. No part of this publication may be reproduced,
stores in a retrieval system, or transmitted in any form or by any means
without the prior permission in writing of Carrot House.

Printed : First published January 2019
　　　　　Reprinted September 2019

Author : Carrot Language Lab

ISBN 978-89-6732-292-2

Printed and distributed in Korea
9F, 488, Gangnam St. Gangnam-gu, Seoul, 06120, South Korea

Curriculum Map

Course	Level 1	Level 2	Level 3	Level 4	Level 5	Level 6	Level 7	Text Book
General Conversation	Essential English: Begin Again							
	Pre Get Up to Speed 1-2							
		New Get Up to Speed+ 1-2						
			New Get Up to Speed+ 3-4					
				New Get Up to Speed+ 5-6				
					New Get Up to Speed+ 7-8			
		Daily Focused English 1						
		Daily Focused English 2						
Discussion				Active Discussion 1				
					Active Discussion 2			
						Dynamic Discussion		
			Chicken Soup Course					
				Dynamic Information & Digital Technology				
Business Conversation	Pre Business Basics 1							
		Pre Business Basics 2						
			Business Basics 1					
				Business Basics 2				
					Business Practice 1			
						Business Practice 2		
Global Biz Workshop				Effective Business Writing Skills (Workbook)				
				Effective Presentation Skills (Workbook)				
					Effective Negotiation Skills (Workbook)			
					Cross-Cultural Training 1-2 (Workbook)			
				Leadership Training Course (Workbook)				
Business Skills				Simple & Clear Technical Writing Skills				
				Effective Business Writing Skills				
				Effective Meeting Skills				
				Business Communication (Negotiation)				
				Effective Presentation Skills				
					Marketing 1			
						Marketing 2		
						Management		
On the Job English				Human Resources				
				Accounting and Finance				
				Marketing and Sales				
				Production Management				
				Automotive				
				Banking and Commerce				
				Medical and Medicine				
				Information Technology				
				Construction				
			Construction English in Use 1~4					
			Public Service English in Use					

※ This Curriculum Map illustrates the entire line-up of textbooks at CARROT HOUSE.

CARROT HOUSE_ 2019.01

new+
GET UP TO SPEED
Situational

Introduction

Carrot House Methodology

Andragogical Approach & Productive English
The teaching of children (pedagogy) and adult learning (andragogy) are distinctively different. Pedagogy is akin to training and encourages convergent thinking and rote learning. It is compulsory, centered on the teacher and the imparting of information with minimal control by the learner. Andragogy, by contrast, is about education as freedom. It encourages divergent thinking and active learning. It is voluntary, learner oriented and opens up vistas for continual learning. Adults need to feel independent and in control of their learning. Therefore, Carrot House curriculum is based on andragogy and is designed to encourage learners' participation and engagement by providing more task-based activities and opportunities to frequently interact in the classroom. People want to achieve communicative competence when they learn other languages. English education in EFL environments has been rather focused on the receptive skills of English—listening and reading—which simply increases learners' knowledge about a language, not the competence of using it. If people are well equipped with productive skills—speaking and writing—they will be competent in English communication. This is why Carrot House curriculum is designed to enhance learners' productive skills throughout the course. This andragogical approach of the Carrot House Curriculum, which focuses on productive English, will enable learners to achieve communication skills necessary for global competence. Carrot House's teaching philosophy and curriculum combine to provide a "Language for Success" for all learners.

Communicative Language Learning (CLL)
This communicative interaction, the essential component of language acquisition, does not occur in a typical, non-meaningful, fun-oriented conversation with native speakers. It occurs in a negotiated interaction through which a well-trained teacher provides the comprehensible input that is appropriate to the learners. The learners, at the same time, actively utilize the opportunities given to them by the teachers. To this end, the Communicative Language Learning (CLL) method is employed in the field of Foreign Language Acquisition. The CLL method provides activities that are geared toward using language pragmatically, authentically and functionally with the intention of achieving meaningful purposes.

Course Overview

Features

Productive English
Learn to use practical and authentic expressions in various daily conversation, common collocations, written sentences, and activities.

Maximization of Schema
The use of visual texts, topic specific questions and useful expressions allow learners to find connections between the contents and their lives by maximizing their schema.

Interactive Activity
Activities, such as role-play, pair-work, group-work, and class-work, provide learners with the opportunity to constantly interact each other.

A Range of Everyday Topics
Through dealing with a range of daily situations in class, learners are equipped to tackle similar situations in reality.

Discussion
Learners can expand their ability to effectively express themselves in English through discussing a broad range of topics.

Slang / Idiom
Through learning topic-related slang and idioms, learners can improve their English language proficiency and use contemporary informal expressions to articulate their ideas.

Opinions on Topic-related Situations
Aims to enhance learner's abilities to speak logically. This task gives learners the chance to express their opinions on a given topic or from a choice of two situations.

Lesson Composition

Each New Get Up To Speed+ Situational book is composed of 12 lessons. Each lesson is composed of 7 main activities and 5 useful extra activities.

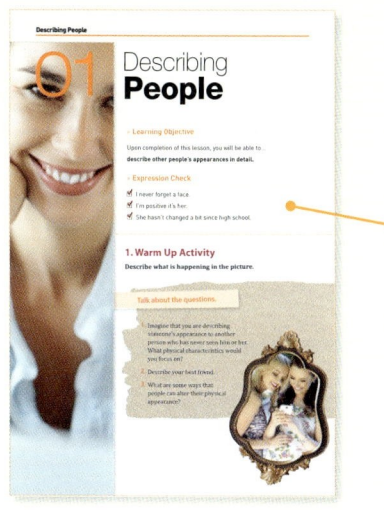

1. Warm Up Activity

To activate the students and their background knowledge, the lesson starts with discussing an image together with three situation-related-questions.

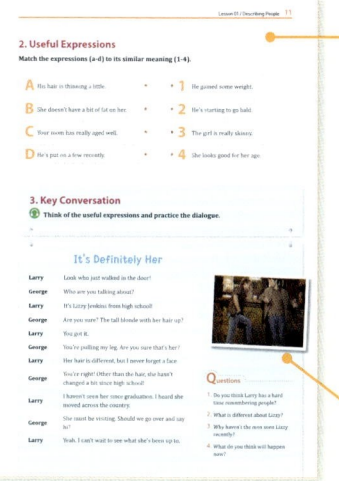

2. Useful Expression

Students can expand their English-language ability by practicing actively used expressions in various situations.

3. Key Conversation

Students can read, listen, and repeat how native speakers communicate with others on a daily basis. The activity also includes questions to test comprehension skills.

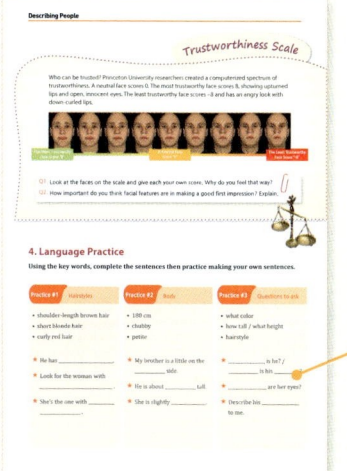

4. Language Practice

Students can practice using key words and expressions to complete sentences and create their own sentences. This helps students to apply and remember what they have learned.

Lesson Composition

Each New Get Up To Speed+ Situational book is composed of 12 lessons. Each lesson is composed of 7 main activities and 5 useful extra activities.

5. Role Plays

Task-based role plays puts off the burden of acting but focuses on the language and task achievement and ability to express oneself in various situations.

6. Cultural Discussion Questions

Gives the learners the opportunity to share, learn, and discuss global, cultural, and personal opinions and notions.

7. Slang & Idioms

Reinforce the learner's ability to speak English like a native through the use of situational contemporary slang & idioms.

Extra Activities

Each lesson includes five extra activities: three engaging facts and figures, Situational Collocations, and Did You Know?. These activities provides students with both popular and intriguing global facts. These can also be used to help facilitate a more fun and enjoyable class.

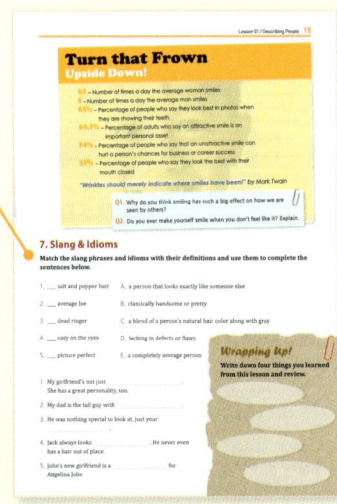

Contents

Title	Learning Objective	Expression Check	
Lesson 1 Describing People	To describe other people's appearance in detail.	- I never forget a face. - I'm positive it's her. - She hasn't changed a bit since high school.	10
Lesson 2 The Great Outdoors	To discuss outdoor activities and experiences.	- Do you think the weather is going to hold out? - I hear that… is great this time of year. - There is nothing like being in the great outdoors.	16
Lesson 3 My New Wardrobe	To buy new clothes at retail stores.	- Where are the new arrivals? - Which ones are on sale? - Are these buy-one-get-one-free?	22
Lesson 4 Where Should We Go?	To make suggestions about what to eat and decide on a restaurant with others.	- Where do you feel like going? - Have you tried that new Irish pub? - What do you say we hit up Joe Cool's?	28
Lesson 5 Moving Up in the World	To congratulate others and discuss professional achievements.	- Congratulations on your new promotion. - I couldn't be any prouder of you. - Let's celebrate your new promotion.	34
Lesson 6 Hitting The Gym	To discuss the importance of fitting exercise into a busy schedule.	- I'd like to make it to the gym today. - I don't have the energy to work out. - I have time to squeeze in a quick workout.	40
Lesson 7 House Hunting	To discuss the features of a home.	- What's the square footage of this place? - We'd like to put in an offer. - We've got a $20,000 down payment.	46
Lesson 8 Making Dinner Reservations	To make dinner reservations over the phone.	- Could I make a reservation, please? - Do you have any tables available for 7:00 p.m.? - How many people is the reservation for?	52
Lesson 9 Sports and Games	To discuss and predict the outcome of sporting events.	- I think the home team is going to win today. - I'm betting on Spain to take it all. - It should be a close game.	58
Lesson 10 Banking	To do personal banking at a local bank.	- I'd like to deposit this money into my savings account, please. - Could you please put this toward my credit card? - Would you mind confirming a transaction for me?	64
Lesson 11 Thanks, But No Thanks	To decline an invitation without hurting other people's feelings.	- Thanks anyway, but I'm not into that. - I'd like to, but… - Can I take a rain check?	70
Lesson 12 Making a Doctor's Appointment	To call a doctor's office and schedule an appointment.	- Would it be possible to make an appointment today? - Could you come at 4:00 p.m. this afternoon? - Could you squeeze me in today?	76

Slang & Idioms — 82

Answer Key — 84

Describing People

01 Describing People

» Learning Objective

Upon completion of this lesson, you will be able to...

describe other people's appearances in detail.

» Expression Check

- ☑ I never forget a face.
- ☑ I'm positive it's her.
- ☑ She hasn't changed a bit since high school.

1. Warm Up Activity

Describe what is happening in the picture.

Talk about the questions.

1. Imagine that you are describing someone's appearance to another person who has never seen him or her. What physical characteristics would you focus on?

2. Describe your best friend.

3. What are some ways that people can alter their physical appearance?

Lesson 01 / Describing People

2. Useful Expressions

Match the expressions (a-d) to its similar meaning (1-4).

A His hair is thinning a little. ★   ★ 1 He gained some weight.

B She doesn't have a bit of fat on her. ★   ★ 2 He's starting to go bald.

C Your mom has really aged well. ★   ★ 3 The girl is really skinny.

D He's put on a few recently. ★   ★ 4 She looks good for her age.

3. Key Conversation

🎧 Think of the useful expressions and practice the dialogue.

It's Definitely Her

Larry	Look who just walked in the door!
George	Who are you talking about?
Larry	It's Lizzy Jenkins from high school!
George	Are you sure? The tall blonde with her hair up?
Larry	You got it.
George	You're pulling my leg. Are you sure that's her?
Larry	Her hair is different, but I never forget a face.
George	You're right! Other than the hair, she hasn't changed a bit since high school!
Larry	I haven't seen her since graduation. I heard she moved across the country.
George	She must be visiting. Should we go over and say hi?
Larry	Yeah. I can't wait to see what she's been up to.

Questions

1. Do you think Larry has hard time remembering people?
2. What is different about Lizzy?
3. Why haven't the men seen Lizzy recently?
4. What do you think will happen now?

Describing People

Trustworthiness Scale

Who can be trusted? Princeton University researchers created a computerized spectrum of trustworthiness. A neutral face scores 0. The most trustworthy face scores 8, showing upturned lips and open, innocent eyes. The least trustworthy face scores –8 and has an angry look with down-curled lips.

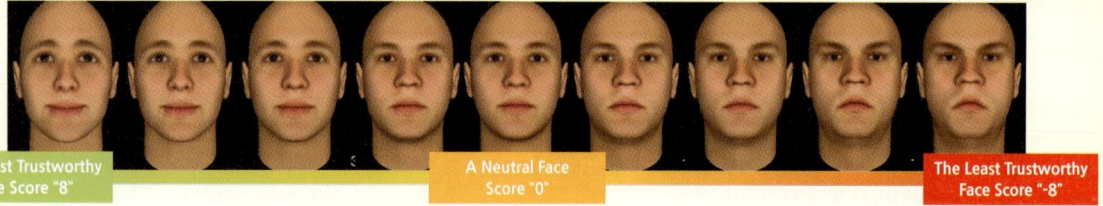

The Most Trustworthy Face Score "8"   A Neutral Face Score "0"   The Least Trustworthy Face Score "-8"

Q1. Look at the faces on the scale and give each your own score. Why do you feel that way?

Q2. How important do you think facial features are in making a good first impression? Explain.

4. Language Practice

Using the key words, complete the sentences then practice making your own sentences.

Practice #1 — Hairstyles

- shoulder-length brown hair
- short blonde hair
- curly red hair

★ He has _____.

★ Look for the woman with _____.

★ She's the one with _____.

Practice #2 — Body

- 180 cm
- chubby
- petite

★ My brother is a little on the _____ side.

★ He is about _____ tall.

★ She is slightly _____.

Practice #3 — Questions to ask

- what color
- how tall / what height
- hairstyle

★ _____ is he? / _____ is his _____?

★ _____ are her eyes?

★ Describe his _____ to me.

5. Role Plays

Look at the situations and act out the role plays with your partner.

Situation #1

Role A
You are new to a city and don't know anyone. A friend from your hometown arranged for you to have dinner with his cousin that lives there. Find each other in a busy area by describing yourself on the phone.

1. Say why you are calling.
2. Describe your clothing.
3. Describe your appearance.

Role B
Your cousin asked you to show one of his friends around your city. You have never met this person before.

1. Ask how you can find him or her.
2. Ask about his or her physical appearance.
3. Greet him or her in person.

Role A
_____ just stole your wallet! Help police find the thief by describing his appearance.

1. Tell when and where the crime occurred.
2. Give the officer an approximate height and weight of the thief. Describe any unique facial features.
3. Describe what the thief was wearing.

Role B
You are a police officer helping a victim of a robbery. Get a description of the thief to complete a report about the incident.

1. Ask about the thief's appearance.
2. Ask about the thief's clothing.
3. Promise to do your best to help.

Situation #2

Situational Collocations!

Look at the collocations and try making your own sentences.

striking appearance	The actress who attended the Academy Awards had a very striking appearance.
jet-black hair	I used to have jet-black hair when I was younger.
going bald	I can see that my father is going bald now.
get pierced	Can I please get my ears pierced tomorrow?
wear makeup	Should schools allow students to wear makeup?
broad shoulders	His broad shoulders show how hard he works out every day.
sleek hair	She has beautiful sleek, shoulder-length hair.
pointed face	Her mom has a pointed face but her dad has a round face.

1.
2.

Describing People

Quick Ways to Improve Your Appearance

Please put a check mark beside each item that applies to you.

- ☐ Get into the habit of drinking more water.
- ☐ Get enough sleep.
- ☐ Wake up and go to sleep at the same times every day.
- ☐ Wear things that compliment your body shape.
- ☐ Exercise at least 3-5 times a week.
- ☐ Stretch every day to improve flexibility.
- ☐ Maintain good posture.
- ☐ Make eye contact with people; do not look at the floor.
- ☐ Always smile.

Q1. Are there any special things you do to improve your appearance?

Q2. Do you think it is necessary for people to try hard to improve their appearances? Why or why not?

6. Cultural Discussion Questions

Talk about the questions in as much detail as possible.

1. How have your culture's beauty standards changed over the years? Explain.
2. Is cosmetic surgery popular in your country? If yes, which procedures are the most common?
3. What are some things that people do to change their appearances in your country?
4. In your opinion, is it a good idea to judge people based on their appearances? Explain.

Did You Know?

Read and discuss how you feel about each fact.

1. Did you know that a typical woman changes her hairstyle more than *100* times during her lifetime?
2. Did you know that *64 percent* of people believe their appearance has helped them get assistance from a stranger?

Turn that Frown Upside Down!

62 – Number of times a day the average woman smiles

8 – Number of times a day the average man smiles

63% – Percentage of people who say they look best in photos when they are showing their teeth

99.7% – Percentage of adults who say an attractive smile is an important personal asset

74% – Percentage of people who say that an unattractive smile can hurt a person's chances for business or career success

23% – Percentage of people who say they look the best with their mouth closed

"Wrinkles should merely indicate where smiles have been!" by Mark Twain

Q1. Why do you think smiling has such a big effect on how we are seen by others?

Q2. Do you ever make yourself smile when you don't feel like it? Explain.

7. Slang & Idioms

Match the slang phrases and idioms with their definitions and use them to complete the sentences below.

1. ___ salt and pepper hair   A. a person that looks exactly like someone else

2. ___ average Joe   B. classically handsome or pretty

3. ___ dead ringer   C. a blend of a person's natural hair color along with gray

4. ___ easy on the eyes   D. lacking in defects or flaws

5. ___ picture perfect   E. a completely average person

1. My girlfriend's not just _____. She has a great personality, too.

2. My dad is the tall guy with _____.

3. He was nothing special to look at, just your _____.

4. Jack always looks _____. He never even has a hair out of place.

5. John's new girlfriend is a _____ for Angelina Jolie.

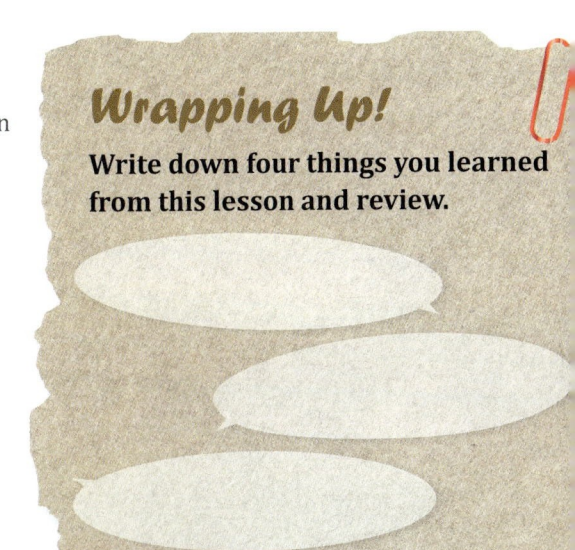

Wrapping Up!
Write down four things you learned from this lesson and review.

02 The Great Outdoors

» **Learning Objective**

Upon completion of this lesson, you will be able to...
discuss outdoor activities and experiences.

» **Expression Check**

- ☑ Do you think the weather is going to hold out?
- ☑ I heard that ... is great this time of year.
- ☑ There is nothing like being in the great outdoors.

1. Warm Up Activity

Describe what is happening in the picture.

Talk about the questions.

1. Do you prefer indoor activities or outdoor activities?
2. What are your favorite outdoor activities?
3. Where is your favorite place to go when you want to be outside? What do you do there?

Lesson 02 / The Great Outdoors 17

2. Useful Expressions

Match the expressions (a-d) to its similar meaning (1-4).

A Do you think the weather is going to hold out?

B There's nothing like being in the great outdoors.

C I heard that the beach is great this time of year.

D Did you bring all of the gear?

1 Did you pack everything we'll need?

2 This season is the perfect time to go to the beach.

3 I really enjoy being outside.

4 Will the weather stay nice?

3. Key Conversation

Think of the useful expressions and practice the dialogue.

Hiking on Whistler

Beth	There's nothing like being in the great outdoors.
Rick	Do you want to go for a hike tomorrow?
Beth	Where did you have in mind?
Rick	I heard that Whistler is great this time of year.
Beth	Whistler, hmmm? Do you think the weather is going to hold out?
Rick	According to the Weather Channel, it's supposed to be sunny and warm all week.
Beth	That's great news.
Rick	So, you want to go?
Beth	Yes. Provided you help me finish with the garden today.
Rick	It's a deal.

Questions

1. Do you think Beth and Rick enjoy being outside?
2. Do you think they are active people?
3. Why do you think Rick wants to go to Whistler?
4. What do you think they will do now?

The Great Outdoors

Don't Forget to Warm Up

Warming up is an important part of physical activities. Muscle stiffness can lead to muscle injury, so try to complete a warm up aimed at loosening up muscles before beginning any physical activity. You can find an example of a basic warm up below:

- *Jogging (5–10 minutes) to increase body temperature*
- *Dynamic stretching exercises (10–15 minutes) to reduce muscle stiffness*

4. Language Practice

Using the key words, complete the sentences then practice making your own sentences.

Practice #1 — Types of activities	Practice #2 — Discussing planned activities	Practice #3 — Interrupted plans
• hiking • skiing • gardening	• climb / Mt. Everest • kayak / the Amazon River • go snorkeling / the Great Barrier Reef	• for a run / snow • skiing / warm • hiking / rain
★ You have to go _____ in the winter. ★ Summer is the best time for _____ . ★ I enjoy _____ in the autumn.	★ We're going to _____ on _____ . ★ They're planning to _____ _____ . ★ Will you _____ at _____ ?	★ We went _____, but we had to turn around because it started to _____. ★ The boys planned to go _____ , but it was too _____ . The snow wouldn't stick. ★ I was going to go _____, but it started to _____ .

5. Role Plays

Look at the situations and act out the role plays with your partner.

Role A

The weather is amazing today and you want to go on a hike. Call a friend to see if he or she wants to join you.

1. Greet your friend and ask what he or she is doing.
2. Ask if your friend wants to go hiking.
3. Discuss where your friend wants to go.

Role B

You are bored at home when a friend calls. You feel like doing something outside, but you don't know what.

1. Say you aren't busy.
2. Accept the invitation.
3. Decide on a location and a meeting place together.

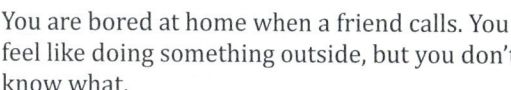

Role A

You and a friend are planning a summer trip. You both enjoy outdoor activities. Decide what to do together.

1. Ask your friend about his or her favorite summer activities.
2. Suggest a location to do that activity.
3. Plan what equipment you will need.

Role B

You and a friend are planning a trip. Discuss what outdoor activities you could do together.

1. Discuss summer activities to find something you both enjoy.
2. Agree on a location to do that activity.
3. Decide who will be responsible for packing specific pieces of equipment.

Situational Collocations!

Look at the collocations and try making your own sentences.

overnight journey	It's an overnight journey but you may not want to sleep.
field trip	I went on a school field trip to Jeju Island.
leisure time	What do you usually do during your leisure time?
goose bumps	I was covered in goose bumps from seeing that sight.
meaningful experience	I'm glad to hear that you had such a meaningful experience.
depressing weather	It is such a cold and depressing weather today.
quite the climb	The mountain is very steep, so its going to be quite the climb.
by foot	We need to to cross the mangrove by foot to get to the hot springs.

1.
2.

The Great Outdoors

What's Inside Your First Aid Kit?

If you are planning an outdoor activity, it is a good idea to bring a first aid kit. A basic first aid kit should include:

- **Adhesive bandages** in all sizes
- **Non-stick gauze** to cover larger wounds
- **Adhesive tape** to help secure the gauze
- **An antibiotic ointment** to prevent infections in a wound or minor burn
- **Elastic bandages** to wrap and provide compression for sprains and strains
- **Ice packs** for when an injury first occurs
- **Tweezers** for removing splinters
- **Thermometer** for checking for fever
- **Eye wash** for removing dirt and dust from the eyes
- **Anti-bacterial hand spray** for keeping your hands clean at all times without needing any water

6. Cultural Discussion Questions

Talk about the questions in as much detail as possible.

1. What are some popular activities to do each season in your country?
2. Which season is your favorite for outdoor activities? Explain.
3. Where is your favorite place to go when you want to be outdoors? What do you do there?
4. What are some things that you need to think about when planning an outdoor activity?

Did You Know?

Read and discuss how you feel about each fact.

1. Did you know that **51% of hospital emergency room** visits in the US are a result of injuries caused by outdoor activities?
2. Did you know that **snowboarding** is the leading cause of sports injuries in the US?

Lesson 02 / The Great Outdoors 21

Adventurous Outdoor Activities

Bungee Jumping
Bungee jumping is a well-known extreme sport. To bungee jump, you essentially tie yourself to a rubber band and leap from a bridge or crane only to bounce back up.

Skydiving
When skydiving, the diver will jump from a plane thousands of feet above the ground, with nothing but a piece of thin material (the parachute) to slow his or her fall.

Mountain Biking
Mountain biking is a sport involving riding specially adapted bicycles off-road. Mountain bikes are similar to other bikes but include features that enhance their durability and performance on rough terrain.

7. Slang & Idioms

Match the slang phrases and idioms with their definitions and use them to complete the sentences below.

1. ___ weather / cooperate with us   A. to prepare an area for sleeping outside

2. ___ run out of gas   B. to begin a journey

3. ___ get away from it all   C. to run out of energy

4. ___ set up camp   D. for weather will be like one hopes for

5. ___ hit the trail   E. to escape from everyday life

1. I love going camping. It's great to _____.

2. I hope that the _____ will _____.

3. That flat spot over there looks like a good place to _____.

4. Whenever you are ready, we can head out and _____.

5. After all of that walking, I think I've _____.

Wrapping Up!

Write down four things you learned from this lesson and review.

1. _____
2. _____
3. _____
4. _____

My New Wardrobe

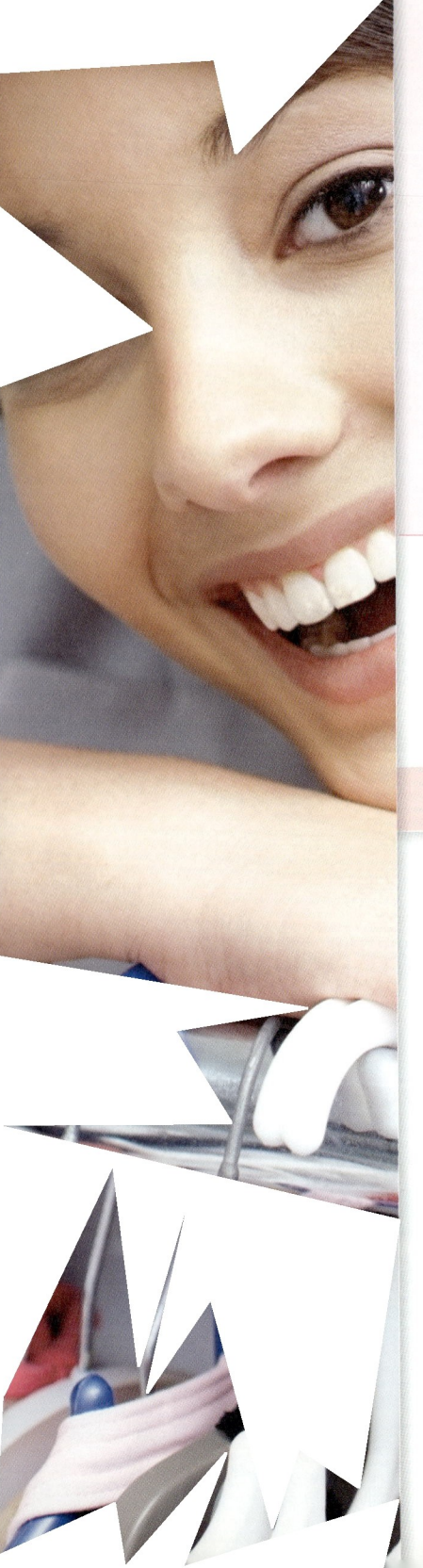

My New Wardrobe

» Learning Objective

Upon completion of this lesson, you will be able to...
buy new clothes at retail stores.

» Expression Check

- ☑ Where are the new arrivals?
- ☑ Which ones are on sale?
- ☑ Are these buy-one-get-one-free?

1. Warm Up Activity

Describe what is happening in the picture.

Talk about the questions.

1. What items of clothing do you have the most of in your wardrobe?
2. Do you consider yourself fashionable? Why or why not?
3. Describe the outfit you are wearing today.

2. Useful Expressions

Match the expressions (a-d) to its similar meaning (1-4).

A Where are the new arrivals?

B Which ones are on sale?

C Are these buy-one-get-one-free?

D Do you want me to open a fitting room for you?

1 Are these two for the price of one?

2 Are you ready to try those on?

3 Which items are discounted?

4 Can you point me to the new spring collection?

3. Key Conversation

 Think of the useful expressions and practice the dialogue.

Shopping for Clothes

Madison Excuse me. Can you point me to the new arrivals?

Saleswoman Of course. Right this way. We have some lovely floral dresses that just came in for spring.

Madison They're gorgeous! But a little out of my price range.

Saleswoman We have a lot of items on sale today for our seasonal clearance.

Madison I'm really just looking for some jeans today.

Saleswoman We have a large selection over here, and today they are buy-one-get-one-free.

Madison I really like these. Do you have any other sizes? I think I need a size up.

Saleswoman Yes, I'll see what we have in the back. Would you like me to open a fitting room for you?

Madison Yes, thanks. My arms are getting tired already!

Saleswoman Sure. It's room 6 when you're ready.

Questions

1. Do you think the saleswoman was helpful?

2. Why did the saleswoman offer Madison a fitting room?

3. What do you think Madison will do now?

4. Do you always try on clothing before buying it? Why or why not?

My New Wardrobe

Clothing Patterns

We often buy clothes based on the pattern of the fabric. Let's learn the names of some common patterns.

**Which patterns do you buy most often?
Are you wearing any patterns right now?**

1. solid
2. striped
3. polka-dotted
4. plaid
5. print
6. checked
7. floral
8. paisley

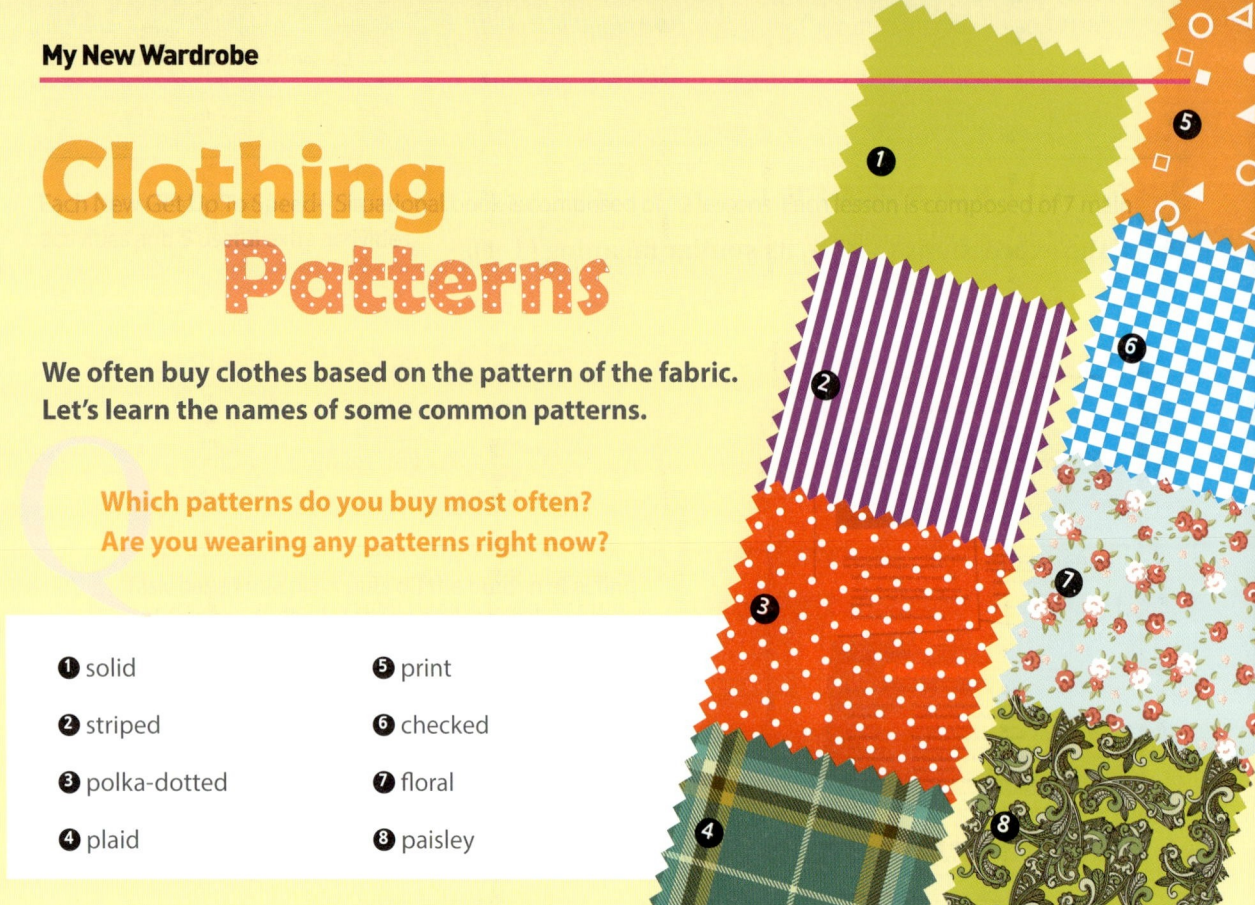

4. Language Practice

Using the key words, complete the sentences then practice making your own sentences.

Practice #1 — Sale	Practice #2 — Asking for other options	Practice #3 — In the fitting room
• on sale • on clearance • 50% off	• another size • different color • other lengths	• flattering • make me look fat • look too long

★ Are there any graphic T-shirts _____ yet?

★ Are the skinny jeans still going to be _____ this weekend?

★ Do you have any button-down shirts _____ today?

★ These pants are a little long. Do they come in _____ _____ ?

★ This skirt is too big. Could you bring me _____ ?

★ Is this jacket available in a _____ ?

★ Do you think these pants _____ ?

★ I'm not sure about this. Are you sure it's _____ ?

★ Do these jeans _____ to you?

5. Role Plays

Look at the situations and act out the role plays with your partner.

Situation #1

Role A

You are a salesperson in a sporting goods store. Help a customer pick out an appropriate jacket for his or her vacation plans.

1. Offer your help to the customer.
2. Ask what features the customer is interested in.
3. Show the customer several jackets.

Role B

You are shopping for a jacket to use on a fall camping trip. You need something waterproof and lightweight that will still be warm at night. Getting a good deal is important to you.

1. Explain that you are looking for a jacket.
2. Tell what kind of jacket you want.
3. Ask if there are any on sale.

Situation #2

Role A

You are shopping with a friend at a busy sale. The line for the fitting rooms is really long and you don't want to lose your place by going to get another item.

1. Ask your friend to come and look at what you are wearing.
2. Explain what you don't like about it.
3. Ask your friend to bring you another item. Thank your friend.

Role B

You and a friend are shopping for clothes. Your friend has just tried something on in the dressing room and wants your honest opinion and help.

1. Ask your friend wants instead.
2. Suggest another item for your friend to try that he or she might like better.
3. Ask questions to make sure you bring the right size and color.

Situational Collocations!

Look at the collocations and try making your own sentences.

last-minute shopping	I'm going to the mall to do some last-minute Christmas shopping.
terrible taste	He has terrible taste in clothing.
shopping spree	My wife enjoyed her little shopping spree at the mall after a big project.
picked up bargains	I picked up a few good bargains at the thrift store.
hit the mall	I'm going to hit the mall after class to do some winter shopping.
on sale	I usually buy my electronics when they are on sale.
window shopping	I can learn new fashion trends through window shopping.
impulse buying	You need to learn to control your impulse buying.

1.
2.

My New Wardrobe

Do You Enjoy Online Shopping?

More and more people are buying their clothes online. There are some advantages and disadvantages to shopping online.

 Advantage
- You can shop 24 hours a day.
- Goods are often cheaper.
- You are able to read reviews written by other people who have purchased the item.
- You can compare as many products and prices as you want.

 Disadvantage
- You do not get to try things on!
- Shipping costs add to how much you are paying for each item.
- Clothing ordered online takes quite a bit of time to get to you.
- You don't support your local businesses and economy as much.

Q Do you usually buy clothes online? Why or why not? What have you bought online recently?

6. Cultural Discussion Questions

Talk about the questions in as much detail as possible.

1. In your opinion, where is the best place to go shopping for clothing in your city? Why?
2. Do you think it is important to think about where an item was made when buying clothing? Why or why not?
3. Do you prefer to shop for clothing alone or with someone? Why do you feel that way?
4. When purchasing clothing, which is more important to you, quality or price? Explain.

Did You Know?

Read and discuss how you feel about each fact.

1. Did you know that *71%* of shoppers surveyed believe they can get a *better deal online* than in stores?
2. Did you know that an average of *28%* of shoppers will *abandon items* in their online shopping cart if they feel that shipping costs are too high?

Q Do you prefer to shop at popular apparel brand stores or local apparel store? Why?

Which brand store do you prefer to buy your clothes from? Why?

7. Slang & Idioms

Match the slang phrases and idioms with their definitions and use them to complete the sentences below.

1. ___ BOGO
2. ___ slashed its prices
3. ___ fast fashion
4. ___ dry clean only
5. ___ a steal

A. an approach to the production of clothing that makes trends quickly and cheaply available in stores
B. to clean with chemicals that have little or no water
C. to greatly reduce the cost of an item
D. a bargain
E. buy one, get one free

1. This dress is such _____ ! I can't believe how much I'm saving today!
2. The store has _____ because they are going out of business.
3. The shoes today are _____, so we can both get a pair.
4. _____ retailers are putting many local stores out of business with their stylish designs and low prices.
5. Don't put that in the wash! It's _____.

Wrapping Up!

Write down four things you learned from this lesson and review.

1
2
3
4

04 Where Should We Go?

» Learning Objective

Upon completion of this lesson, you will be able to...

make suggestions about what to eat and decide on a restaurant with others.

» Expression Check

- ☑ Where do you feel like going?
- ☑ Have you tried that new Irish pub?
- ☑ What do you say we hit up Joe Cool's?

1. Warm Up Activity

Describe what is happening in the picture.

Talk about the questions.

1. Which do you prefer - a home-cooked meal or eating out at a restaurant?
2. What factors do you think about when choosing a restaurant?
3. Do you enjoy trying new restaurants, or do you prefer to eat at places that you know you will enjoy? Why?

2. Useful Expressions

Match the expressions (a-d) to its similar meaning (1-4).

A. What do you feel like having this evening?

B. What do you say to Mexican?

C. Why don't we just eat out tonight?

D. Let's grab a bite to eat after work.

1. Do you want to go out for dinner?

2. Do you feel like eating Mexican?

3. Let's get something to eat when we are finished with work.

4. What are you in the mood to eat tonight?

3. Key Conversation

Think of the useful expressions and practice the dialogue.

How About Dinner?

Laura Hey, Ginny, how are you doing? It's been ages!

Ginny Oh yes, it has! What have you been up to?

Laura Why don't we go somewhere and catch up over dinner?

Ginny I think that's a wonderful idea! What do you feel like having? Chinese? Japanese? Italian?

Laura What do you say to Mexican? There's a new place down the street, and the tacos are to die for!

Ginny That sounds great! I'll try anything once! Let's go!

Laura It's too early. They open in an hour.

Ginny How about grabbing a drink at Larry's Cantina while we're waiting? Does that suit you?

Laura That's fine with me.

Questions

1. How do you think they know each other?

2. Who do you think is more familiar with the area?

3. Do you like Laura's suggestion?

4. What kind of food would you have picked?

Where Should We Go?

Rating a Restaurant

There are many things that customers look for when choosing a restaurant. Four of the most important ones are listed below:

1. Atmosphere/Ambiance
2. Cleanliness
3. Service
4. Food

Q. Based on the four factors, evaluate a restaurant you recently visited by circling your level of satisfaction for each quality.

	Unsatisfied				Satisfied
Atmosphere/Ambiance	1	2	3	4	5
Cleanliness	1	2	3	4	5
Service	1	2	3	4	5
Food	1	2	3	4	5

Q. What else do you consider when choosing a restaurant? Write down your answers below.

5. .... , 6. ....

4. Language Practice

Using the key words, complete the sentences then practice making your own sentences.

Practice #1 — Choosing food

- Chinese food
- Thai food
- fast food

★ Would you be OK with _____ ?

★ Is _____ all right with you?

★ How does _____ sound to you?

Practice #2 — Suggesting

- hit up
- catch up over dinner
- grabbing a drink

★ How about _____ while we are waiting?

★ Why don't we go somewhere and _____ ?

★ What do you say we _____ that new Mexican restaurant?

Practice #3 — Expressing feelings

- to die for
- try anything once
- in the mood for

★ I've never had that, but I'll _____ .

★ I'm _____ a big, juicy steak.

★ The tacos at that restaurant are _____ .

5. Role Plays

Look at the situations and act out the role plays with your partner.

Situation #1

Role A

You run into an old high school classmate on the street. You want to catch up with him or her.

1. Greet your friend and ask what he or she is doing.
2. Ask questions about his or her food preferences.
3. Suggest a restaurant.

Role B

You run into an old friend from high school and ask them to go to lunch.

1. Say that you don't have any plans and ask if he or she wants to eat lunch.
2. Choose a kind of food.
3. Agree to eat where your friend suggests.

Situation #2

Role A

Your coworker just helped you out with a tough assignment at work. You want to treat him or her to dinner.

1. Thank your coworker and offer to take him or her out to dinner.
2. Offer up three choices.
3. Ask questions about your coworker's preferences to choose a restaurant.

Role B

Your coworker wants to buy you dinner. You don't eat meat. Discuss where you want to go to eat.

1. Agree to go to dinner tonight.
2. Explain that your dietary restrictions.
3. Agree on a place to eat.

Situational Collocations!

Look at the collocations and try making your own sentences.

strongly suggest	I strongly suggest you take these medications.
rave reviews	The new Italian restaurant down the street has been receiving rave reviews.
lost appetite	You seem to have lost your appetite. Let me take you to a nice restaurant.
group lunch	My boss requested me to make a reservation for group lunch.
spacious dining room	At Boston BBQ, meals are served family-style in the spacious dining room.
tough choices	Everyone faces tough choices in their lives.
light meal	I'm not so hungry, so I would like to grab a light meal.
strong preference	Many people expressed a strong preference for the original plan.

1. ....

2. ....

Where Should We Go?

6. Cultural Discussion Questions

Talk about the questions in as much detail as possible.

1. In your country, what are the most popular kinds of restaurants to go to after work with colleagues?
2. Is it rude to turn down a dinner invitation in your culture? Explain.
3. What kinds of restaurants do you think are the best for entertaining overseas visitors?
4. Recommend a restaurant you enjoy to your class. Where is it? What do they serve?

When you are choosing a restaurant to celebrate a special occasion, how do you find the best place to go? Here are some common ways people find restaurants.

- ☑ **Use a Smart Phone** – *Apps for Foodies*
- ☑ **Search the Internet** – *Blogs for Foodies*
- ☑ **Ask Friends for Recommendations**

Q. How do you usually find a new restaurant?

Did You Know?

Discuss how you feel about each fact.

1. Did you know which fast food chain is the biggest in the US? By number of restaurants? *Subway.* By total revenue? *McDonald's.*
2. Did you know that there are nearly **41,000 Chinese restaurants** in the US, three times the number of McDonald's franchises?

Lesson 04 / Where Should We Go? 33

Not for the First Date!

If you want to make a good first impression on your **first date**, then you had better be careful what you eat!

Q1. Which do you think is better to eat on a first date - spaghetti or a steak? Why?

Q2. Which do you think is better to eat on a first date - a hamburger or sushi? Why?

7. Slang & Idioms

Match the slang phrases and idioms with their definitions and use them to complete the sentences below.

1. ___ you are what you eat
2. ___ call ahead
3. ___ on an empty stomach
4. ___ wined and dined
5. ___ order in

A. without eating anything
B. to call in advance
C. eat good food in order to be healthy
D. to order delivery food from a restaurant
E. to try to impress someone with an expensive meal

1. Maybe we should take a break and eat something. I don't think well _____.

2. He was _____ by the company until he agreed to work there.

3. Do you really want fast food again? You know they say, _____.

4. That place has gotten really popular lately. I'll _____ and make sure they have a table for us.

5. I'm too tired to even think about cooking. Do you want to just _____ tonight?

Wrapping Up!
Write down four things you learned from this lesson and review.

1.
2.
3.
4.

Moving Up in the World

» Learning Objective

Upon completion of this lesson, you will be able to...
congratulate others and discuss professional achievements.

» Expression Check

- ☑ Congratulations on your new promotion.
- ☑ I couldn't be any prouder of you.
- ☑ Let's celebrate your new promotion.

1. Warm Up Activity

Describe what is happening in the picture.

Talk about the questions.

1. How are promotions decided at your company? Explain.
2. Have you ever been promoted? If so, how did it make you feel?
3. What are some things that people can do to increase their chances of receiving a promotion?

2. Useful Expressions

Match the expressions (a-d) to its similar meaning (1-4).

A Enjoy your new corner office.

B I guess your hard work hasn't gone unnoticed!

C I guess you're making the big bucks now.

D You're climbing the corporate ladder quickly.

1 You're being promoted quickly inside your company.

2 You're making really good money now.

3 Your new office will have a great view.

4 People notice and appreciate your efforts.

3. Key Conversation

Think of the useful expressions and practice the dialogue.

You Deserve It

John: Did you all hear the fantastic news about Mr. Daniels?

Joyce: What are you talking about, John? What's this fantastic news?

John: I can't believe you haven't heard. Mr. Daniels has been promoted to Division Head.

Lynn: Ahh…Why didn't you tell us, Mr. Daniels?

Mr. Daniels: Well, I just heard about it myself.

Lynn: Congratulations, Mr. Daniels! Nobody deserves it more than you.

Mr. Daniels: Thank you very much. I have all of you to thank for it. Without you, it would have never happened.

Joyce: We all need to go out tonight to celebrate Mr. Daniels's promotion.

John: Most definitely.

Mr. Daniels: I had better get back to work, or they will take that promotion away from me. I'm leaving this in your capable hands.

Questions

1. How do the others feel about Mr. Daniels's promotion?
2. Do you think news travels quickly in their office?
3. How do you think they will celebrate Mr. Daniels's promotion?
4. How might Mr. Daniels feel now?

Moving UP the Ladder

While it is not realistic that you will be promoted as quickly as you hope, there are some tactics you can use to improve your chances.

✓ **Act Professionally at All Times**
- **Dress neatly and professionally** even on business casual days.
- **Ask questions when you are not sure** how to do something.
- **Dare to be different** – **make yourself stand out** from the pack.
- **Keep a positive outlook** on things even in tough situations.
- **Do not whine, complain, or blame** others even though things do not go your way.
- **Make a name for yourself** in your industry through conferences, articles, and speeches.
- Do not be a clock-watcher.

✓ **Be a Problem-solver**
- Being a "go-getter" who is willing to throw his hat into the ring for any task shows gumption.
- **Do not go to your boss with problems.** If a difficult situation arises, be sure to come up with at least one solution before seeking your boss's blessing for dealing with the situation.

✓ **Keep a Strong Network**
- **Knowing the right people** can give you access to information around the office.
- **Have a mentoring relationship** with someone higher in the company.

4. Language Practice

Using the key words, complete the sentences then practice making your own sentences.

Practice #1 — Congratulating

- Congratulations on your promotion.
- Your promotion is well deserved.
- You certainly earned your promotion

★ A: _____ .
  B: I appreciate that. Thanks for the support.

★ A: _____ .
  B: Thank you very much. I'm very excited about it.

★ A: _____ .
  B: Thanks. It was a long time coming.

Practice #2 — Stating an accomplishment

- promotion / CEO
- transferred / overseas
- promotion / Division Head

★ Well done on your _____ to _____ .

★ Great job getting _____ _____ .

★ Congratulations on your _____ to _____ .

Practice #3 — Offering praise

- Nobody deserves it more than you do.
- We couldn't be any prouder of you.
- You are definitely the right man for the job.

★ A: They just told me that I've been promoted to manager.
  B: _____ .

★ A: I'm going to be transferred overseas.
  B: _____ .

★ A: I just heard that I've been promoted.
  B: _____ .

5. Role Plays

Look at the situations and act out the role plays with your partner.

Situation #1

Role A
One of your closest co-workers has just been promoted to Department Head. Now, he will be your boss. Offer him your congratulations.

1. Tell your co-worker congratulations.
2. Praise him or her on this well-deserved promotion.
3. Offer to take him or her out to celebrate.

Role B
You were just promoted to Department Head! You are on your way to a meeting when a co-worker stops to congratulate you.

1. Thank your co-worker.
2. Accept the invitation.
3. Say you need to leave for a meeting.

Role A
You just received a promotion and a job transfer to an overseas branch. You are very excited, but you only have two weeks to prepare for your move. You can't wait to share your good news with your teammates.

1. Tell about your promotion and move.
2. Talk about how you will miss working together.
3. Accept the offer to celebrate.

Role B
Your teammate was just promoted to a higher position in an overseas branch. Congratulate him or her and make plans to celebrate the promotion before he or she leaves.

1. Congratulate your teammate on the promotion.
2. Offer to take your coworker out to celebrate before his or her move.
3. Promise to make plans later.

Situation #2

Situational Collocations!

Look at the collocations and try making your own sentences.

make a profit	At that price, can we still make a profit?
launch a product	He will definitely be promoted because he successfully launched a new product this year.
hard work	The promotion paid off for all the hard work.
bright idea	The new marketing manager has a box full of bright ideas.
rewarding job	For me, teaching is a very rewarding job.
glittering career	She has a glittering career ahead of her.
earn a fortune	They only have a few long-term clients, but they earn a fortune.
responsible position	You are too young for such a responsible position.

1.
2.

Moving Up in the World

Compliment Your Boss

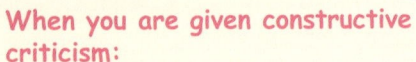

Here are three tips you can give to compliment your boss without looking like you are trying too hard.

When you are praised for a job well done:
"Thank you for recognizing my part in this assignment, but we never could have achieved this outcome without your guidance."

When you are given constructive criticism:
"I really appreciate the time you've taken to give me this opportunity to learn under you."

When a task is being explained to you by your boss:
"I never thought of doing it that way – what a great idea!"

6. Cultural Discussion Questions

Talk about the questions in as much detail as possible.

1. Do you think that people should be promoted based on ability or the time they have worked at a company? Why?

2. Is getting a responsible position always a good thing? Explain.

3. How do you celebrate when someone is promoted in your country? Be specific.

4. What are some things that employees can do to improve their chances of being promoted at your company?

Did You Know?

Read and discuss how you feel about each fact.

1. Did you know that studies show *79 percent* of people who quit their jobs claim *'lack of appreciation'* as their reason for leaving?

2. Did you know that *the #1 strategy* for getting promoted is mentoring under someone higher in the company who can help to *spread the good word* about you?

WHERE TO SIT?

Where you sit in a meeting matters A LOT. Do you want to be noticed? Do you want to stealthy? Do you need to leave early? Here's how to pick the perfect place to sit in a meeting.

A: Power Player This seat is for the boss or person leading the meeting.
B & C: Allies / Flanking Positions These seats are for those who support the boss or want to be heard and noticed.
D: The Middles This seat is for those who only want to listen and not be noticed.
E: The Contender Typically, this seat will be noticed the most and taken by the person with the opposing opinion.
F: Sideliners This seat is for people who need to be stealthy, leave early, or in the meeting as an assistant.

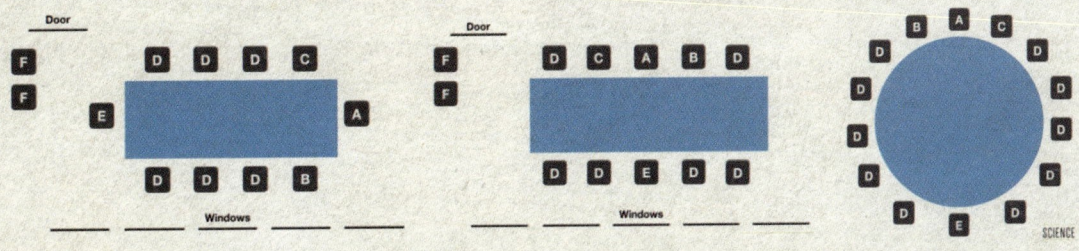

Tip! The left side is more noticed by the Power Player. If you want to be less noticed, sit on the right.

7. Slang & Idioms

Match the slang phrases and idioms with their definitions and use them to complete the sentences below.

1. ___ on top of the world
2. ___ This calls for a celebration!
3. ___ making bank
4. ___ word on the street
5. ___ head honcho

A. to earn a large amount of money
B. happy and elated
C. the highest ranking person
D. We should celebrate!
E. a rumor or piece of information currently being circulated

1. The _____ is that John is going to be made team leader.
2. I guess you are the new _____ of the department.
3. I've been _____ since I heard that I'm getting promoted.
4. You should buy this round since you are _____ now.
5. I just heard the good news! _____

Wrapping Up!

Write down four things you learned from this lesson and review.

Hitting the Gym

06 Hitting the Gym

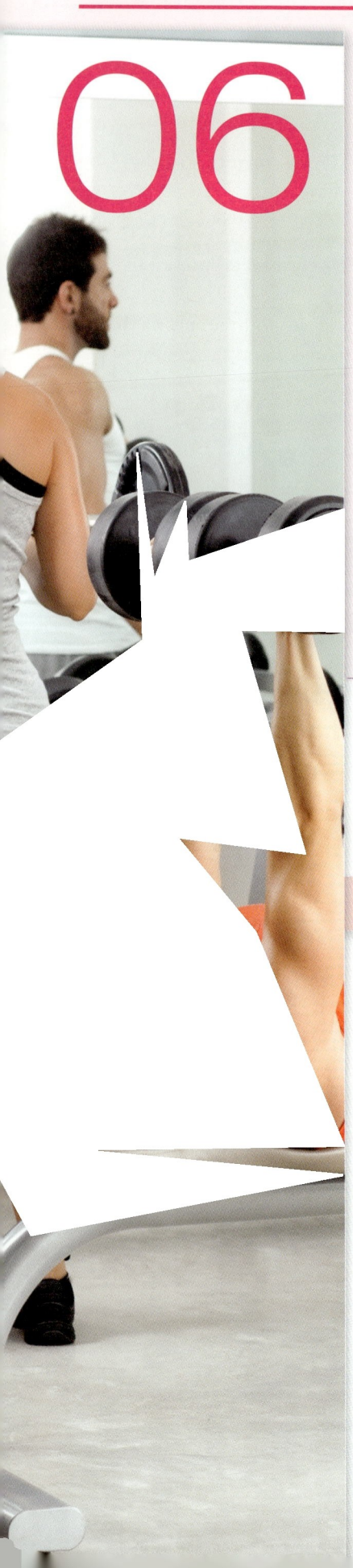

» Learning Objective

Upon completion of this lesson, you will be able to…
discuss the importance of fitting exercise into a busy schedule.

» Expression Check

- ☑ I'd like to make it to the gym today.
- ☑ I don't have the energy to work out.
- ☑ I have time to squeeze in a quick workout.

1. Warm Up Activity

Describe what is happening in the picture.

Talk about the questions.

1. Is exercise an important part of your lifestyle? Explain.
2. Is joining a gym expensive in your country?
3. What kinds of exercise do you enjoy? Where do you do them?

2. Useful Expressions

Match the expressions (a-d) to its similar meaning (1-4).

A I'm starting to become a couch potato.

B I feel like pumping iron today.

C Hitting the gym will give me my second wind.

D I'm getting so out of shape.

1 Going to the gym gives me a lot of energy.

2 I'm not in a good physical condition lately.

3 I feel like I'm spending too much time in front of the television.

4 I'm in the mood to lift weights today.

3. Key Conversation

Think of the useful expressions and practice the dialogue.

I feel out of shape!

Frank Hi, honey, what are you doing?

Diana Hey, you're calling late. Are you still at work?

Frank Yes, but I'm just leaving. I was thinking of hitting the gym, but I don't have the energy to work out.

Diana Well, maybe you should skip going to the gym today.

Frank I'd love to, but I haven't been to the gym in two weeks. I feel really out of shape these days.

Diana Why don't you just have a quick workout and come home?

Frank Yeah, good idea. I'll pump some iron and hit the treadmill for a quick run.

Diana You always get your second wind after you exercise.

Frank OK, I'll hurry, and we can do something when I get home.

Diana Sounds great. Have a good workout, and see you soon.

Questions

1. Why do you think Frank is so tired today?
2. What do you think Frank and Diana's relationship is?
3. Do you think Frank will feel like doing something after his workout?
4. Do you normally feel energized after a workout?

Hitting the Gym

Top 3 Commonly Broken New Year's Resolutions

1 Lose Weight and Get Fit

One research study says that 60% of gym memberships go unused and attendance is usually back to normal by mid-February.

2 Quit Smoking

Only an estimated 15% of people who try to quit manage to stay cigarette-free six months later.

3 Learn Something New

Resolving to learn something new is exciting. But, soon people remember there is a reason they have not learned it before. They say they will do it when they have more time.

Q1. What were your New Year's Resolutions this year?
Q2. Did you successfully keep your resolutions?

4. Language Practice

Using the key words, complete the sentences then practice making your own sentences.

Practice #1 — Workout

- hit the gym
- work out
- go for a swim

★ I'm going to _____ during lunch.

★ I need to _____ after work.

★ I like to _____ before work.

Practice #2 — At the gym

- stretching
- do strength training
- run on the treadmill

★ I go to the gym to just to _____.

★ I like to start by _____.

★ I _____ to build more muscles.

Practice #3 — Excuses and goals

- lifting weights
- going to the gym
- exercise before work

★ A: I just don't have time to exercise these days.
B: Why don't you _____?

★ A: I'm too skinny.
B: Try _____ to add muscle.

★ A: I'm starting to feel like a couch potato.
B: You should start _____.

Lesson 06 / Hitting the Gym 43

5. Role Plays

Look at the situations and act out the role plays with your partner.

Situation #1

Role A
You want to start exercising but you have a hard time motivating yourself to go alone. Try to convince a co-worker to go to the gym with you.

1. Explain your problem to your coworker.
2. Discuss what time of day you would like to go together.
3. Agree and suggest a gym near your office.

Role B
You've been feeling out of shape lately and have been complaining about it to a coworker. Make plans to join a gym together.

1. Explain why joining a gym would be good for you.
2. Suggest working out in the morning.
3. Make plans to meet tomorrow.

Situation #2

Role A
You and a friend are having coffee. Your friend just started working out. Compare your fitness routines.

1. Ask how the gym is going.
2. Choose an activity that you also enjoy and talk about it.
3. Agree to meet to do that activity and decide on a place to do it.

Role B
You joined a gym last month and are very excited about your new workout routine.

1. Tell about your favorite activities.
2. Suggest you do one together sometime.
3. Discuss what equipment you will need to prepare.

Situational Collocations!

Look at the collocations and try making your own sentences.

fitness equipment	You should know how to use fitness equipment properly for your safety.
toned body	She has such a perfectly toned body. I'm so jealous!
gain weight	Some people gain weight after they stop smoking.
moderate exercise	Moderate exercise is necessary for good health.
train hard	Before they enter a competition, athletes train hard.
lame excuse	Stop making lame excuses. You really need to start working out.
break sweat	I always break a sweat when I go to dance class.
gym membership	I have a gym membership at a 24-hour fitness center.

1.
2.

Hitting the Gym

6. Cultural Discussion Questions

Talk about the questions in as much detail as possible.

1. What are some of the current fitness trends in your country?

2. What are some ways to get exercise other than going to a gym in your area?

3. In your opinion, are people in your country generally healthy? Why do you think so?

4. Do you have a regular exercise routine? Where do you exercise?

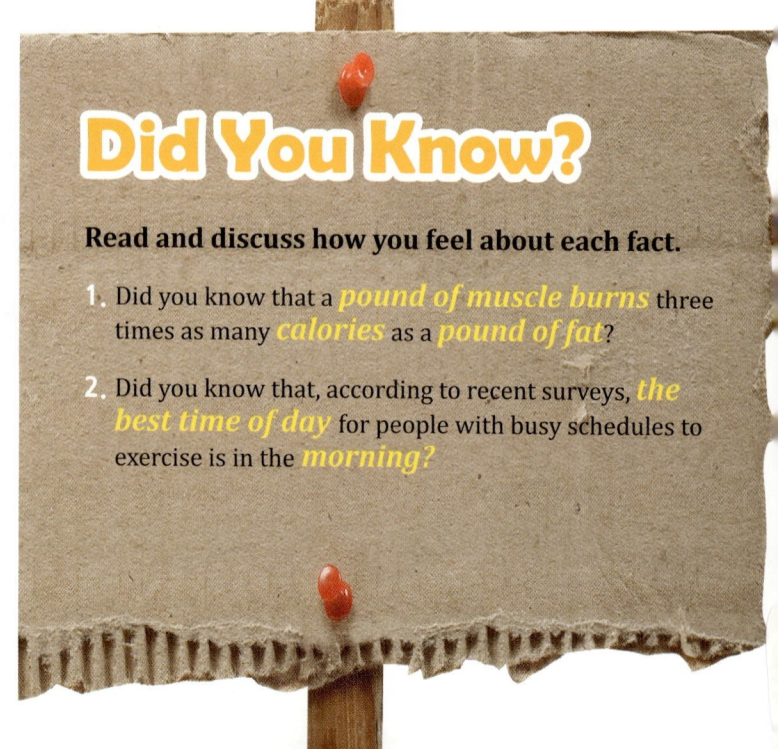

What's Best for You?
Running, Yoga, or Swimming?

Running, swimming, and yoga are all great exercises to incorporate into your workout, but which one is right for you?

1 Running
Running is an exercise that you can do anywhere in any kind of weather with the right apparel. If you are not an outdoorsy type, you can run on a treadmill.

2 Swimming
Swimming is the perfect aerobic exercise if you have to be easy on your joints or you are just getting back into exercise after suffering an injury.

3 Yoga

If you are looking for a low impact and relaxing workout, yoga is a great exercise. It will help with flexibility, endurance, and balance.

Q Which one do you think is the best for you? Why?

7. Slang & Idioms

Match the slang phrases and idioms with their definitions and use them to complete the sentences below.

1. ___ get in a workout
2. ___ swim some laps
3. ___ spare tire
4. ___ burn off
5. ___ drop a few pounds

A. a roll of fat around a person's waist
B. to get rid of energy or fat through exercise
C. to swim the length of a pool repeatedly
D. to lose weight
E. to fit exercise in a tight schedule

1. I'd really like to _____ before my vacation.
2. I lost my _____ through a lot of hard work at the gym.
3. I'm going to the gym to try to _____ some of that pizza I had for lunch.
4. I try to wake up early to go to the gym and _____ before work.
5. I think I'll _____ at the pool after work tonight.

Wrapping Up!
Write down four things you learned from this lesson and review.

1.
2.
3.
4.

House Hunting

07

House
Hunting

» Learning Objective

Upon completion of this lesson, you will be able to...

discuss the features of a house.

» Expression Check

- ☑ What's the square footage of this place?
- ☑ We'd like to put in an offer.
- ☑ We've got a $20,000 down payment.

1. Warm Up Activity

Describe what is happening in the picture.

Talk about the questions.

1. Have you even been house or apartment hunting before? Describe your experience.
2. Is it difficult to find a house to buy in your area?
2. What is your current house like, and how does it compare to your dream house?

2. Useful Expressions

Match the expressions (a-d) to its similar meaning (1-4).

- **A** What's the square footage of this place?
- **B** We'd like to put in an offer.
- **C** We've got a large down payment.
- **D** I'm looking for a studio.

- **1** I'd like an apartment with one room.
- **2** We can pay a lot upfront.
- **3** How large is this home?
- **4** We want to make a bid on this place.

3. Key Conversation

Think of the useful expressions and practice the dialogue.

Making an Offer

Kevin So, this is the place I told you about. Third floor, three bedrooms, two baths, hardwood floors, excellent view.

Brad What kind of upgrades have they done?

Kevin All the fixtures are less than two years old. The master bath has a whirlpool tub.

Brad I like the granite countertops in the kitchen. Could you tell me about the appliances?

Kevin All stainless steel appliances, as you can see. The refrigerator has a built-in water filtration system.

Brad What's the square footage of this place?

Kevin It's 1,350 square feet, not including the balcony.

Brad It's quite spacious. We really want something close to town, so this sure fits the bill.

Kevin Would you like to make an offer?

Brad Yes, and see if they'll throw in the washer and dryer. We'd like to move in as soon as possible.

Questions

1. When is Kevin looking to move?
2. Would you rather buy a recently remodeled home or an older one that you can remodel to meet your needs?
3. What factors do you consider most important when hunting for a home?
4. What features are most important to Brad?

House Hunting

Things to Consider

Here are four categories of things to consider when you buy a house.
What's the most important factor for you?

Size
☆ How big would you like your house to be?
☆ How many bedrooms do you need?
☆ How many bathrooms do you need?
☆ Do you need parking? How many spaces?

Special Features
☆ Do you expect some built-in furniture?
☆ Do you want a storage area?
☆ Do you have any animals that will require special facilities?
☆ Do you have family members with special needs?
☆ Do you want special features to save energy and enhance indoor air quality?

Neighborhood
☆ Do you want to live in an urban, suburban, or rural area?
☆ Do you have to be close to public transportation?
☆ Is being in a good school district important?
☆ Would you like to live close to someone in the same neighborhood?
☆ Is a good view important to you?

Stage of Life
☆ How many children do you have? (If you are planning a family, how many would you like?)
☆ Do you have any adult children who will be moving out soon?
☆ Are you close to retirement?
☆ Do you have an older relative who might come to live with you?

4. Language Practice

Using the key words, complete the sentences then practice making your own sentences.

Practice #1 — How big is it?

- square footage
- dimensions
- floor plan

★ Do you know the _____ of each room?

★ Could I have a copy of the basic _____ , please?

★ What is the total _____ _____ of the property?

Practice #2 — Special features

- kitchen / appliances
- walk-in closet / master
- house / security system

★ I want a _____ with all new _____ .

★ I'd really like a _____ with a _____ installed.

★ A _____ in the _____ bedroom is essential.

Practice #3 — Purchasing a house

- put in an offer / $170,000
- put down / $20,000
- counteroffer / small changes

★ We agree with their _____ , but we would like them to make _____ _____ .

★ We want to _____ _____ .

★ We _____ for _____ .

5. Role Plays

Look at the situations and act out the role plays with your partner.

Situation #1

Role A
You are a single person looking for an apartment. You would like to live within 20 minutes of your workplace. Because you are trying to save money, you want to find the cheapest apartment possible. You are meeting with a realtor for the first time.

1. Greet the realtor and explain why you have come today.
2. Explain the size and location you are interested in.
3. Tell about any special needs you have (pets, parking space, elevator, etc.)

Role B
You are a realtor helping a new customer find an apartment. Ask questions about the customer's preferences to find the best home for him or her.

1. Ask the customer about where they would like to live.
2. Ask about the customer's price range.
3. Ask if the customer needs any special facilities.

Situation #2

Role A
You are asking your older sibling for advice about picking out an apartment. Explain what you need and listen to his or her opinions.

1. Ask what factors you should think about.
2. Talk about what you are looking for in an apartment.
3. Tell about your dream apartment.

Role B
Your younger sibling is looking for his or her first apartment. Give advice on what things to look for.

1. Explain what you think are the most important factors.
2. Ask your sibling questions about his or her specific needs.
3. Offer to help by going with your sibling to the realtor.

Situational Collocations!

Look at the collocations and try making your own sentences.

residential area	The facility is located in a residential area.
fully furnished	This house is fully furnished.
completely refurbished	Each room has been completely refurbished.
move out	The owner wants us to move out by the end of this month.
cramped room	While the office is being renovated, employees have to work in a cramped room.
housewarming party	Thanks for inviting me to your housewarming party.
pleasant surroundings	I wish to work in more pleasant surroundings.
conveniently located	Our office is conveniently located just a few minutes from the station.

1.
2.

House Hunting

What Affects Home Value?

The value of a piece of property includes both the value of the land itself and any improvements that have been made to it. Land values increase when demand for land exceeds the supply of available land, or if a particular piece of land has intrinsic value greater than neighboring areas (e.g. oil can be found on the land).

The following items can affect the value of a home.
- Quiet, safe, clean, attractive neighborhood
- Overall positive public perception of the community
- Adequate fire and police protection
- Quality public schools
- Libraries and other cultural institutions
- Distance from shopping and restaurants
- Access to public transportation
- Well-maintained infrastructure: roads, parks, and other public recreation facilities
- History of solid property values
- Planned or proposed changes to zoning

Q. What areas in your country have the highest real estate prices? Why do you think that is?

Q. What are some factors that influence home values in your country?

6. Cultural Discussion Questions

Talk about the questions in as much detail as possible.

1. Which is more common in your country - buying or renting a home? Explain.

2. Do you think real estate prices in your city are too expensive? Why?

3. Are there any improvements that can increase home value in your country? Explain.

4. Are home prices negotiable where you live?

Did You Know?
Read and discuss how you feel about each fact.

1. Did you know that since the *1970s* the *size* of the average American home has *increased* by more than *1,000 square feet (~93m²)*?

2. Did you know that the median home price in the US is *$220,100*?

Bring Home the Bacon!

Here are some useful idioms using the word 'home'.

Bring home the bacon: (informal) To earn money to live on.

A man's home is his castle: One can do whatever one wants to in one's own home.

Charity begins at home: You should take care of family and people close to you before you worry about helping others. This can also be applied to countries or organizations devoted to spending on foreign aid.

Come in and make yourself at home: Please come into my home and make yourself comfortable.

Men make houses; women make homes: Men are often the ones who build or acquire houses for their families, but women provide the things that make a house into a home.

Feel at home: To feel as if one belongs; to feel as if one were in one's home; to feel accepted.

7. Slang & Idioms

Match the slang phrases and idioms with their definitions and use them to complete the sentences below.

1. ___ fixer-upper
2. ___ asking price
3. ___ have a roof over our heads
4. ___ counteroffer
5. ___ throwing money down the drain

A. the price at which something is offered for sale
B. have a place to live
C. a house in need of repairs
D. an offer made in response to another
E. wasting money

1. We put in a _____ and are waiting on a final decision from the buyer.
2. We want to come in just under the _____ with our offer.
3. This house is a real _____, but I think we got a good deal on it.
4. We'll _____ in a few weeks.
5. Paying extra for facilities we won't use is just _____.

Wrapping Up!

Write down four things you learned from this lesson and review.

Making Dinner Reservations

08 Making Dinner Reservations

» Learning Objective

Upon completion of this lesson, you will be able to...

make dinner reservations over the phone.

» Expression Check

- ☑ Could I make a reservation, please?
- ☑ Do you have any tables available for 7:00 pm?
- ☑ How many people is the reservation for?

1. Warm Up Activity

Describe what is happening in the picture.

Talk about the questions.

1. What are some occasions when you might need to make a dinner reservation?
2. Do you prefer to make dinner plans in advance, or would you rather wait and decide just before the meal?
3. When was the last time you made a dinner reservation? Why did you make it?

2. Useful Expressions

Match the expressions (a-d) to its similar meaning (1-4).

A We're all booked up.

B I've penciled you in.

C How many are in your party?

D I'll set one aside for you.

1 I'll save one for you.

2 I wrote down your name for that time slot.

3 There are no tables available at this time.

4 How many people will be joining you?

3. Key Conversation

🎧 **Think of the useful expressions and practice the dialogue.**

Calling Ahead

Maitre d'	(answering a phone) Thank you for calling Bon Appétit. How may I help you?
Patron	Hi. Could I make a reservation for Friday, please?
Maitre d'	This Friday? I'm sorry; we're all booked up. How about a week from Friday?
Patron	The 20th? Hmmm. I guess that's OK. Do you have any tables available for 7:00 pm?
Maitre d'	We do! How many people is the reservation for?
Patron	Five. Two adults and three kids. Do you have any high chairs?
Maitre d'	Yes, we do. I'll set one aside for you. Could I get your name and cell phone number, please?
Patron	Thanks a lot! Sure. It's Thompson, and the number is 555-7826.
Maitre d'	Great! I've penciled you in for 7:00 pm on the 20th. See you then!
Patron	Thanks again.

Questions

1. Do you think the restaurant is busy?
2. Who do you think is joining the patron for dinner?
3. Did the patron have any problems making a reservation?
4. Why do you think the patron made the reservation?

Making Dinner Reservations

World's Most Expensive Restaurants

01 Ithaa, Maldives

The world's first underwater restaurant is Ithaa in the Maldives. It cost $5 million to create. The interior is an incredible tunnel in the sea, surrounded by fish, coral, rays, and even sharks.

02 Masa, New York

Masa in New York is the most expensive restaurant, costing up to $680 per person. There's no menu. Chef Masa Takayama prepares seasonal food nightly for a unique dining experience.

Q1. What is the most expensive meal that you have ever eaten? Where did you enjoy it?

Q2. Are there any restaurants that are famous for being expensive in your country? What do they serve?

4. Language Practice

Using the key words, complete the sentences then practice making your own sentences.

Practice #1 — Availability

- tables / 7:00 p.m.
- tomorrow night
- private rooms

★ Does your restaurant have _____ available for dinner?

★ Do you have any _____ for _____?

★ What's your availability like for _____?

Practice #2 — Reservations

- make a reservation
- fully booked
- reserve a table

★ I'm sorry, but we are _____ _____ for dinner tonight.

★ Could I _____ for five?

★ I'd like to _____ for six people.

Practice #3 — Special requests

- party platters
- booster seats
- booth

★ Do you have any _____?

★ Could we be seated in a _____?

★ Are _____ available at your restaurant?

Lesson 08 / Making Dinner Reservations

5. Role Plays

Look at the situations and act out the role plays with your partner.

Situation #1

Role A

You forgot to make a dinner reservation for your best friend's birthday today. You promised your friend a special night out and don't want to disappoint him. Call a restaurant to try to schedule a reservation.

1. Call the restaurant and ask if there are any tables available.
2. Confirm that you want the reservation the manager offers.
3. Let the manager know about your special event.

Role B

You are the manager of a busy restaurant. You are normally fully booked but tonight you had a cancellation at 8:00 p.m.

1. Inform the caller that there is one table available tonight.
2. Ask for the caller's name, phone number, and the number of people in the party.
3. Promise to bring out a free dessert for the person celebrating a birthday.

Situation #2

Role A

You are responsible for arranging a business dinner for your team and some important clients. You would like to book a private room to make it easier to talk. Call a restaurant to make a reservation.

1. Explain why you are calling.
2. Request a private room.
3. Provide the information requested and thank the speaker for his or her help.

Role B

You are a restaurant employee. Answer the phone and take the customer's reservation.

1. Ask for the desired time and number of diners.
2. Confirm the reservation by asking for the caller's name and number.
3. Repeat the reservation information and thank the customer for calling.

Situational Collocations!

Look at the collocations and try making your own sentences.

fully booked	All the outdoor seats are fully booked.
seasonal menu	Starbucks will launch a new seasonal menu this winter.
check availability	I'm calling to check for table availability.
take reservations	Sorry, we don't take any reservations.
advance booking	We recommend advanced booking for the holidays.
double check	Let me double check your reservation.
operation hour	Our operation hour is Monday to Friday, from 8am to 10pm.
side order	I'd like to the porterhouse with a side order of grilled vegetables.

1.
2.

Making Dinner Reservations

6. Cultural Discussion Questions

Talk about the questions in as much detail as possible.

1. Is it common for restaurants to require reservations in your country?
2. Are online reservation systems common where you live? Have you ever used one?
3. What are the peak hours for dinner reservations in your country?
4. Are there any dates or holidays when it is more difficult to make a dinner reservation in your country? Explain.

Did You Know?

Read and discuss how you feel about each fact.

1. Did you know that dinner reservations in some restaurants at *Walt Disney World* must be booked **180 days in advance**?

2. Did you know that **Mother's Day** is the *busiest day* of the year for restaurants and **Valentine's Day** is the *busiest night*?

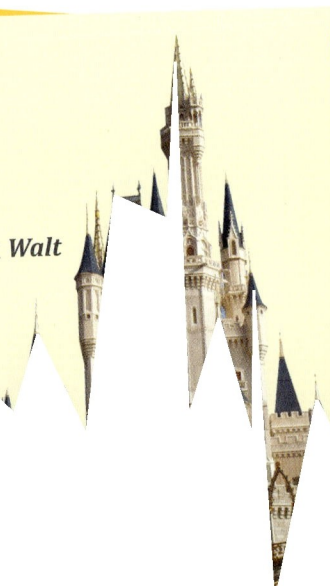

Smoking? Nonsmoking?

Currently, many countries are banning indoor public smoking, but there are still places where smoking is permitted. Here are some questions you might find useful.

"Is this a nonsmoking establishment?"

"Do you have a smoking section here?"

"Is smoking allowed?"

"Is there a designated smoking area?"

Q1. Has your country banned indoor public smoking? If so, when?

Q2. Do you think that smoking should be allowed in public places? Why or why not?

7. Slang & Idioms

Match the slang phrases and idioms with their definitions and use them to complete the sentences below.

1. ___ no show
2. ___ booked solid
3. ___ wasn't a seat in the house
4. ___ waiting list
5. ___ last resort

A. no available seats
B. to be fully reserved
C. a final course of action, used only when all else has failed
D. a person who makes a reservation but fails to come or cancel it
E. a list of people waiting for something

1. I put our name down on the _____, but it will probably be another 30 minutes.

2. Even though we made a reservation, we arrived to find out there _____.

3. The restaurant thought we were a _____, so they gave our table away.

4. The restaurant was packed with people, so my _____ was to have dinner at the bar.

5. I called the restaurant to make a reservation, but they were _____.

Wrapping Up!

Write down four things you learned from this lesson and review.

1. _____
2. _____
3. _____
4. _____

Sports and Games

Sports and Games

» Learning Objective

Upon completion of this lesson, you will be able to...

discuss and predict the outcome of sporting events.

» Expression Check

- ☑ I think the home team is going to win today.
- ☑ I'm betting on Spain to take it all.
- ☑ It should be a close game.

1. Warm Up Activity

Describe what is happening in the picture.

Talk about the questions.

1. Do you prefer watching sports on TV or in person? Why?
2. Which do you prefer: individual or team sports? Explain.
3. Who is your favorite team or athlete?

2. Useful Expressions

Match the expressions (a-d) to its similar meaning (1-4).

A. I think the national team is going to win today.

B. I'm betting on Spain to take it all.

C. The Bears are going to school them today.

D. It should be a close match.

1. I think this game belongs to the national team.
2. The score will almost be even.
3. I think they are going to win.
4. I think they're going to show the other team who's boss.

3. Key Conversation

Think of the useful expressions and practice the dialogue.

We're Going to Take It Tonight!

Miranda Ooh! Score! Your team is SO going down!

James Yeah, well, the game's off to a rocky start, but we're going to take you. Just watch!

Miranda I don't think so. You guys are getting schooled today.

James Nah, this game's going to be tight. Both teams are strong, and there's no point in crying about it yet.

Miranda It's going to be a close match for sure, but I'm betting on Spain to take it all.

James Really? I think Argentina's got a stronger lineup this year, and they were awesome in the semi-finals.

Miranda Shh, we're missing the game. What? Why did he get yellow carded?

James Yeah, didn't you see that foul? It looked like he interfered with number 6.

Miranda Well, if your team keeps playing like that, we're going to be getting a lot of penalty kicks.

Questions

1. Do you think Miranda is a big soccer fan?
2. Which team does Miranda support?
3. Which team does James think is going to win?
4. In your opinion, who seems more confident in their team?

Sports and Games

Sports Trivia

- **A baseball** has exactly **108 stitches**.
- **A soccer ball** is made up of **32 leather panels**.
- The tennis term **"love"** is derived from "l'oeuf," the French word for "egg," **symbolizing zero**.
- **The longest tennis match** took place at Wimbledon 2010. It lasted **11 hours and 5 minutes**.
- **Golf** is the only sport played **on the moon**. On February 6, 1971, Alan Shepard hit a golf ball on the moon's surface.
- **Boxing** became a legal sport **in 1901**.
- **Fishing** is the most participated-in sport in the world.

4. Language Practice

Using the key words, complete the sentences then practice making your own sentences.

Practice #1 — Describing outcomes

- came in second
- got slaughtered
- ended in triumph

★ The game _____ for Atlanta!

★ The Giants _____ the other day.

★ My team _____ this season!

Practice #2 — Expressing an opinion

- picking / to win
- take it all
- go all the way

★ I bet the Yankees will _____ _____ this season.

★ I'm _____ the Braves _____ this game.

★ I think the Falcons are going to _____ this year.

Practice #3 — Predicting close results

- well-matched
- tight game
- tough call

★ This game is going to be a _____ .

★ It's going to be a really _____ .

★ These two teams are _____ .

5. Role Plays

Look at the situations and act out the role plays with your partner.

Situation #1

Role A

You are watching a baseball game with your friend at a bar. You both support different teams, and you think that your team is much better. Tell your friend what you think.

1. Tell who you think will win.
2. Ask your friend if he or she would be interested in betting on the results.
3. Pretend your team just scored.

Role B

You and a friend are watching baseball in a bar. You think your team will win but you think it is going to be a close game.

1. Argue why you think your team is better.
2. Say that you think the game is too close to bet on.
3. Insist your team will recover.

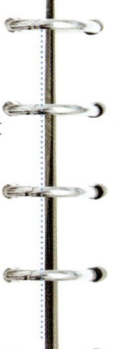

Situation #2

Role A

There is a big soccer game on TV tonight. Make plans with a co-worker who supports a different team to go somewhere to watch it.

1. Ask your co-worker if he or she is interested in watching the game.
2. Discuss a place to watch the game.
3. Predict what the game results will be.

Role B

Your co-worker wants to watch the soccer game tonight. Decide on a place to go to watch.

1. Agree to go and suggest a place you can watch.
2. Make a plan to meet your co-worker after work.
3. Insist your team is going to win.

Situational Collocations!

Look at the collocations and try making your own sentences.

enter a competition	It is hard to persuade her to enter the competition.
enhance performance	This is a great opportunity to enhance my performance.
narrowly defeated	The Bears narrowly defeated the Giants by a single point.
score a goal	He scored a goal with a header.
make a bet	We're going to make a bet on which team wins.
took the lead	The German driver took the lead in the rally.
take first place	Yuna Kim of Korea took first place in figure skating.
compete against	He had to compete against some of the world's best swimmers.

1. ....
2. ....

Sports and Games

Most Expensive Sporting Tickets Ever!

Tennis

1. **Tennis - $67,094**
   2013 Wimbledon Men's Singles Final - Andy Murray vs. Novak Djokovic

2. **Basketball - $59,815**
   2010 NBA Finals - Los Angeles Lakers vs Boston Celtics

3. **Golf - $4,630**
   2013 Master 77th Edition - Adam Scott

4. **Boxing - $31,936**
   2013 "The One" boxing light middleweight championship - Floyd Mayweather Jr. vs Canelo Álvarez

Basketball

6. Cultural Discussion Questions

Talk about the questions in as much detail as possible.

1. Where is your favorite place to watch a sports game on TV? Why?
2. Which sporting events are most popular in your country? When do they occur?
3. How do you feel about betting on sporting events? Explain.
4. Introduce one of your country's most famous athletes. What sport does the athlete play? Why is he or she so famous?

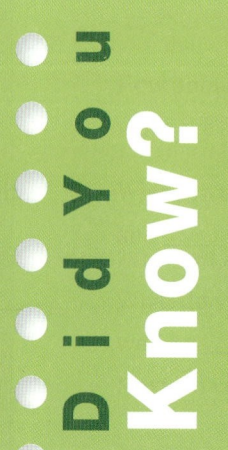

Read and discuss how you feel about each fact.

1. Did you know that the average lifespan of Major League Baseball player is *5-6 years*?

2. Did you know if Michael Phelps were a country, he would rank *#35* on the all-time *gold medal list* ahead of 97 other countries?

Lesson 09 / Sports and Games **63**

World's Top Sport Events

The sports industry is a multi-billion dollar industry where athletes, businessmen, organizations, and even schools take part for the fame, money, and entertainment. Over time, various sporting competitions has grown and generated a value of millions each game.

Super Bowl
$420 million

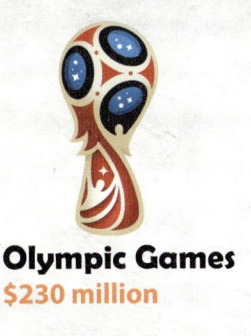

Olympic Games
$230 million

4. UEFA European Football Championship - $110 million
5. Major League Baseball World Series - $106 million
6. Daytona 500 - $100 million
7. Olympic Games (Winter) - $93 million
8. NCAA Men's Final Four - $90 million
9. Major League Baseball All-Star Week - $75 million
10. Kentucky Derby - $67 million

FIFA
$120 million

Q1 How many of the annual sport events listed above do you know? Which ones?

Q2 Are there any sporting events listed above that is not popular in your country? Why do you think so?

7. Slang & Idioms

Match the slang phrases and idioms with their definitions and use them to complete the sentences below.

1. ___ on the edge of my seat
2. ___ a toss-up
3. ___ down to the wire
4. ___ neck and neck
5. ___ throw in the towel

A. to give up
B. a situation whose outcome is not decided until the very last minute
C. even in a race or competition
D. very excited and giving one's full attention to something
E. a situation in which all outcomes or options are equally possible

1. The race is _____, but I think Murphy is pulling ahead.
2. It's getting _____, and there's still no telling who's going to win.
3. It's really _____ as to who's going to take it today.
4. The game was so exciting! I was _____ the whole night!
5. He should just _____ and give up. There's no way he's going to win.

Wrapping Up!

Write down four things you learned from this lesson and review.

1. _____
2. _____
3. _____
4. _____

Banking

10 Banking

» Learning Objective

Upon completion of this lesson, you will be able to...
do personal banking at a local bank.

» Expression Check

☑ I'd like to deposit this money into my savings account, please.
☑ Could you please put this toward my credit card?
☑ Would you mind confirming a transaction for me?

1. Warm Up Activity

Describe what is happening in the picture.

Talk about the questions.

1. Which do you prefer - banking online or in person? Why?
2. How many bank accounts do you currently have? How are they different?
3. How did you choose your current bank?

2. Useful Expressions

Match the expressions (a-d) to its similar meaning (1-4).

A I'd like to make a deposit.

B I just got pre-approved for my loan.

C Do you accept debit?

D I'd like to withdraw some cash.

1 The bank will let me borrow the money.

2 I'd like to pay for this with my bank card.

3 I want to take money out of my account.

4 I want to put money into my account.

3. Key Conversation

Think of the useful expressions and practice the dialogue.

Making a Deposit

Mr. Wilson Good morning. I'd like to deposit this money into my savings account, please.

Teller Sure. Do you have your ATM card with you?

Mr. Wilson No, sorry. I must have forgotten it at home.

Teller No problem. Do you happen to know your account number?

Mr. Wilson Yes. It's 512 3795 411.

Teller Alright. Just a moment. Yes, Mr. Wilson. The money is in the account. Is there anything else I can do for you today?

Mr. Wilson Yes, could you give me a copy of my bank statement from last month?

Teller No problem. Here you go. Will there be anything else?

Mr. Wilson No, thank you.

Teller Have yourself a good day then.

Mr. Wilson You, too.

Questions

1. Why do you think Mr. Wilson does not have his card with him?
2. Do you think Mr. Wilson goes to the bank regularly?
3. Do you think the teller did a good job? Explain.
4. How long do you think Mr. Wilson's transactions would take in real life?

Banking

My Bank Statement

These four items are related to your bank statement.
Discuss what each term means.

1 Deposit

2 Dividend

3 Withdrawal

4 Balance

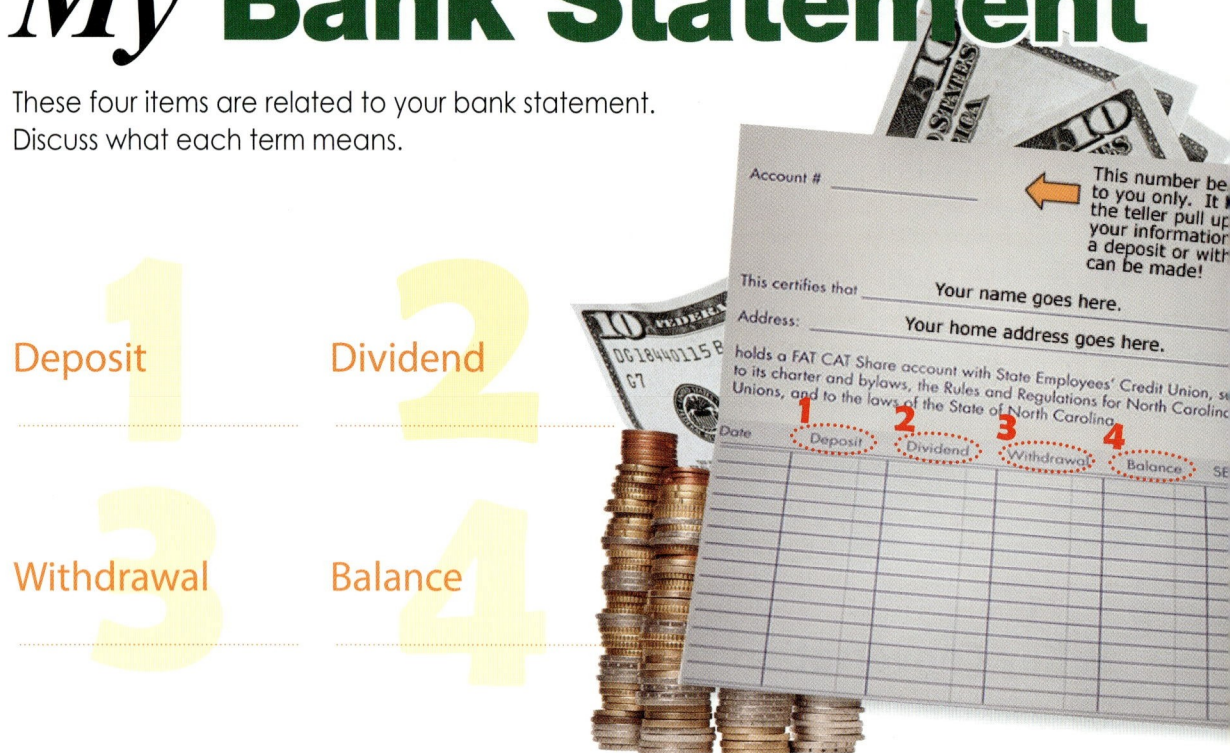

4. Language Practice

Using the key words, complete the sentences then practice making your own sentences.

Practice #1 — Banking

- deposit / checking account
- withdraw / $350
- open / savings account

★ Can I _____ _____ from my account?

★ I'd like to _____ a _____ .

★ Please _____ this into my _____ .

Practice #2 — Applying for a loan

- personal loan
- savings account
- mortgage

★ Can I apply for a _____ _____ , please?

★ How do you apply for a _____ ?

★ How much do you have in your _____ ?

Practice #3 — Documentation

- photo ID
- ATM card
- bank statement

★ Would you like me to print off your _____ ?

★ May I see your _____ , please?

★ Do you have your _____ with you today?

5. Role Plays

Look at the situations and act out the role plays with your partner.

Situation #1

Role A
You are a teller at a bank. Help a customer open a new account.

1. Greet the customer and ask what they would like to do.
2. Ask to see a photo ID and check if he or she would like a debit card.
3. Confirm that the account is opened.

Role B
You just got a new job. Your employer wants you to open an account at a specific bank to deposit your salary into.

1. Explain why you want to open an account.
2. Agree to get a debit card.
3. Thank the teller.

Situation #2

Role A
You just moved and your bank does not have a branch in your new city. Ask your new coworker for advice on choosing a new local bank.

1. Ask your coworker which bank he or she uses.
2. Ask him or her to tell about the advantages of that bank.
3. Ask where the nearest branch is.

Role B
Your coworker just asked you to recommend a bank. Tell your coworker about the benefits of your personal bank and answer his or her questions.

1. Tell your bank name.
2. Describe what you like and dislike about your bank.
3. Give directions to the nearest branch bank from your office.

Situational Collocations!

Look at the collocations and try making your own sentences.

open an account	You need to deposit two-hundred dollars to open your account.
large loan	I was able to get a large loan to open a business.
make a withdrawal	I'd like to make a withdrawal from my savings account.
cost less	It costs less to shop at a hypermarket.
currency exchange rate	Before traveling, check what the currency exchange rate is.
interest rate	The interest rate has dropped suddenly.
personal property	We fully respect personal property rights.
outstanding balance	You have an outstanding balance of five hundred dollars with us.

1.
2.

Banking

What's it Worth?
Fill in the blanks with each coin's value.

A **penny** is worth (1) .... cent(s).
A **nickel** is worth (2) .... cent(s).
A **dime** is worth (3) .... cent(s).
A **quarter** is worth (4) .... cent(s).
A **dollar** is worth (5) .... cent(s).

Who Is on Your Money?
Most paper money is printed with portraits of leaders and other famous people from a nation's history.

I'm George Washington

Who?
Whose portraits are on your country's currency? What did they do?

6. Cultural Discussion Questions

Talk about the questions in as much detail as possible.

1. Do you think interest rates are too high or too low in your country? Explain.
2. Is it easy to open a new bank account in your country? What documents are needed?
3. What is the most common way to pay for things in your country?
4. Are online and mobile banking services popular in your country? What transactions can you use them for?

Did You Know?

Read and discuss how you feel about each fact.

1. The word *mortgage* comes from two Latin words – **"mort," meaning death, and "gage," meaning a pledge** or binding agreement.
2. In 2008, the American government *paid $700 billion* to the major US banks **to avoid a financial crisis.**

Why Did You Choose "That" Bank?

In a recent survey, more than 1,600 people discussed the factors that led them to choose their primary bank.

What do you think is the most common reason for selecting a bank?

❶ 52.6% ❷ 28.9% ❸ 19.7% ❹ 14%

❶ Conveniently located branch or ATM
❷ Past experience or reputation of bank
❸ Recommendation from family or friends
❹ Best interest rate

7. Slang & Idioms

Match the slang phrases and idioms with their definitions and use them to complete the sentences below.

1. ___ froze my account
2. ___ in the red
3. ___ bounced
4. ___ nest egg
5. ___ direct debit

A. a sum of money saved for the future
B. a transaction cannot be processed because of nonsufficient funds
C. an action taken by a bank that prevents any transactions from occurring
D. a payment system where creditors are authorized to charge a customer's bank account directly
E. to have spent more money than one has in an account

1. All of my accounts are _____. I have to find a way to make more money.
2. I set up all my bills to pay by _____, so now I never have to worry about missing a payment.
3. The bank _____ because they noticed some strange charges.
4. The check _____ because there was not enough money in the account.
5. I worked hard and built up a _____ to live comfortably in my retirement.

Wrapping Up!

Write down four things you learned from this lesson and review.

11 Thanks, But No Thanks

» Learning Objective

Upon completion of this lesson, you will be able to...

decline an invitation without hurting other people's feelings.

» Expression Check

- ☑ Thanks anyway, but I'm not into that.
- ☑ I'd like to, but ...
- ☑ Can I take a rain check?

1. Warm Up Activity

Describe what is happening in the picture.

Talk about the questions.

1. Tell about the last time you said no to an invitation. What was your excuse?
2. How might you feel if someone declined your invitation? Explain
3. What are some invitations you will never decline.

2. Useful Expressions

Match the expressions (a-d) to its similar meaning (1-4).

A I'd really like to, but I can't come to your party.

B Can I take a rain check?

C I'm not really into that, but thanks.

D I've got something else on that night.

1 How about another time?

2 I wish I could come to your party.

3 That doesn't interest me much. Sorry.

4 I have other plans.

3. Key Conversation

 Think of the useful expressions and practice the dialogue.

Are You Ditching Me?

Laura I wanted to get back to you about Julie's party this Friday.

Dylan Oh, that's this weekend? I totally forgot, sorry.

Laura Are you seriously ditching me? We talked about that weeks ago!

Dylan My mistake. Hey, to make it up to you, why don't I take you to dinner tomorrow night?

Laura I don't think so. I've got something else going on, and I can't get out of it.

Dylan Well, what about Sunday? We could go hiking over at Stone Mountain Park.

Laura Nah, I'm not really into that, thanks.

Dylan OK, how about you call me after the party, and I'll see if I can swing by your house for a bit?

Laura I think I'll be getting home pretty late. How about another time?

Dylan Well, another time then. I'm sorry about backing out on our plans. Please don't be angry.

Laura I'm not angry. I'm just disappointed.

Questions

1. What do you think about Dylan's character?
2. How do you think Laura feels about Dylan forgetting their plans? Why?
3. If you were Dylan, what would you have done to make it up to Laura?
4. Do you think Laura will forgive Dylan?

Thanks, But No Thanks

How to Say "NO" Nicely

Sometimes you need to say "no" when someone makes a suggestion, offers you something, or asks you to do something for them. Of course, just saying "no" can be rather rude. Here are some of the most common ways to say "no" nicely—or at least not rudely.

- **I'm afraid I can't** go out tonight. I've got a test tomorrow.
- **Sorry, but I don't particularly like** Chinese food.
- **I'd really rather not** take a walk this afternoon.
- **Thank you, but it's not my idea of** a fun afternoon out.
- **Sorry, I'm not really fond of** driving for the fun of it.
- **That's very kind of you, but I really have to** get back to the city.

4. Language Practice

Using the key words, complete the sentences then practice making your own sentences.

Practice #1 — Declining invitations

- something going on
- made other plans
- feeling up to it

★ I hate to say no, but I'm not _____.

★ Sorry, but I've got _____ _____ that night.

★ I'm sorry, but I've already _____ for this weekend.

Practice #2 — Suggesting alternatives

- something else
- some other time
- not into that

★ If you're _____, why don't we make other plans?

★ Could we do _____ instead?

★ Is it OK if we go _____ _____?

Practice #3 — Turning down invitations

- I'm sorry, but I can't make it on Friday.
- Sorry, but can I take a rain check?
- I have other plans that night.

★ A: _____.
B: Ok, how about we do something on Saturday?

★ A: _____.
B: I understand. How about another time?

★ A: _____.
B: No problem. Is everything OK?

Lesson 11 / Thanks, But No Thanks

5. Role Plays

Look at the situations and act out the role plays with your partner.

Situation #1

Role A
You made plans with an old friend to have dinner tonight, but you have to visit your sister in the hospital.

1. Apologize and explain the situation to your friend.
2. Offer to meet again another day.
3. Reschedule your plans to next week.

Role B
You are having dinner with an old friend tonight. You have been looking forward to it for a while.

1. Listen to your friend's problem.
2. Accept your friend's apology and say you understand.
3. Reschedule your dinner plans to next week.

Role A
You made plans to see a movie with your friend, but you just found out your friend invited someone you don't like to join you. Back out of your plans without hurting anyone's feelings.

1. Call your friend and say that something came up.
2. Apologize and make a simple excuse.
3. Promise to make it up to your friend another time.

Role B
You are planning to go to the movies with a friend. Another friend called and invited himself along at the last minute.

1. Say that you are sorry that your friend can't make it.
2. Accept your friend's apology.
3. Promise that you will get together again sometime soon.

Situation #2

Situational Collocations!

Look at the collocations and try making your own sentences.

make it	Sorry for asking, but I don't think I can make it to the party.
make a change	I'm afraid we have to make a change in our plan.
flat refusal	Our requests were met with a flat refusal.
turn down	I can't believe Jenny turned down my invitation.
put off	Never put off until tomorrow what you can do today.
make an excuse	I'm too tired to go out tonight, so let's make an excuse and stay home.
peer pressure	Don't feel peer pressure and just be honest.
deeply sorry	I am deeply sorry for not being available on Friday.

1.
2.

Thanks, But No Thanks

Rain Check?

"This term comes from baseball, where in the 1880s, it became the practice to offer paying spectators a voucher for admission to a future game in exchange for that day's game being cancelled due to rain. This voucher became know as the rain check."

01 If you go to a water park and it starts to rain, they will usually give you a rain check. It's a free pass to come again at a later time (when it is not raining).

02 If you go to a store and want to buy a sale item that is out of stock, you can request a rain check to buy it in the future for the same price.

03 In everyday English, it is something that you say when you cannot accept someone's invitation to do something, but you would like to do it another time.
For example:

- I can't go to the movie tonight, but I'll take a rain check, if that's all right.
- I won't play tennis this afternoon, but can I take a rain check?
- I can't make dinner on Tuesday, but I hope you'll give me a rain check.

6. Cultural Discussion Questions

Talk about the questions in as much detail as possible.

1. Have you ever accepted invitations that you do not want to? Why?
2. In your culture, is it acceptable to be direct about rejections?
3. What do you think are some good reasons for declining an invitation?
4. When you have to decline an invitation, what can you do to avoid hurting the other person's feelings?

Did You Know?

Read and discuss how you feel about each fact.

1. Did you know that there is a *fake phone number* you can give out to *say "no"*? When the person calls the number, he/she will reach the Rejection Hotline, not you!
2. Did you know that a painful rejection can temporarily *reduce a person's IQ by about 25 percent*?

Lesson 11 / Thanks, But No Thanks

Smart Way to **Cancel Plans**

Don't cancel plans unless it's for a very good reason.
Valid Excuses
- you are sick
- your child is sick
- you babysitter suddenly cancelled
- your boss scheduled an unexpected meeting or client

Do it personally
If something comes up, call immediately. Don't text!

Don't give too many details
Too many details make things sound fishy. Make a simple apology.

Don't say "Let's get together soon", if you don't mean it.
No more accepting or making impulsive promises.

Follow up soon
Get back to the person as soon as possible or ask thoughtful questions.

Post responsibly online
If your friend sees you posting about other events on your Facebook or Instagram, you will lose your credibility.

7. Slang & Idioms

Match the slang phrases and idioms with their definitions and use them to complete the sentences below.

1. ___ flake
2. ___ double-booked
3. ___ ditch
4. ___ leave me hanging
5. ___ advance warning

A. to get rid of
B. to keep someone waiting for your decision or answer
C. to accidentally make appointments at a conflicting time
D. notice beforehand
E. an unreliable person

1. I just wanted to give you a little _____ that I can't make it tonight.

2. Let's move to another bar and _____ the boss.

3. Diana is such a _____. She always cancels at the last possible moment.

4. Sorry, but I seem to have _____ myself. I forgot that I'd already promised to have dinner with Jeff tonight when I talked to you earlier.

5. Don't _____ – I need a definite answer by tonight.

Wrapping Up!
Write down four things you learned from this lesson and review.

1. _____
2. _____
3. _____
4. _____

12 Making a Doctor's Appointment

» **Learning Objective**

Upon completion of this lesson, you will be able to...

call a doctor's office and schedule an appointment.

» **Expression Check**

☑ Would it be possible to make an appointment today?
☑ Could you come at 4:00 p.m. this afternoon?
☑ Could you squeeze me in today?

1. Warm Up Activity

Describe what is happening in the picture.

Talk about the questions.

1. When was the last time you visited a doctor? What was wrong?
2. Do you always go to the doctor when you feel sick? Why or why not?
3. Is it easy or difficult to get a doctor's appointment in your country?

2. Useful Expressions

Match the expressions (a-d) to its similar meaning (1-4).

A Could you squeeze me in today?

B Can you pencil me in for two o'clock?

C What does the doctor's schedule look like today?

D Anything works for me.

1 Put me down for 2:00.

2 Is the doctor busy today?

3 Any time will be fine.

4 Do you have any appointments available?

3. Key Conversation

Think of the useful expressions and practice the dialogue.

Is the Doctor Busy Today?

Receptionist	Good morning, Dr. Butler's office. How may I help you?
Patient	Good morning. This is Larry Brown. I'm not feeling so well today. Would it be possible to make an appointment to see the doctor?
Receptionist	Sorry to hear you're under the weather. There is a flu is going around these days, so the doctor is quite busy.
Patient	I don't doubt that for a second. Could you squeeze me in sometime today, please?
Receptionist	Let me see. Could you be here in thirty minutes?
Patient	I don't think I could be there that fast. Do you have anything else available?
Receptionist	All right. Could you come in at half past four this afternoon?
Patient	Yes, that would work just fine.
Receptionist	OK, Larry, so we'll see you at 4:30 p.m. this afternoon.
Patient	Thank you so much for squeezing me in. I really appreciate it. See you later today. Bye for now.
Receptionist	Yes, bye for now.

Questions

1. What might be wrong with Larry?
2. Do you think Larry lives near the doctor?
3. Do you think the doctor will be tired today?
4. Do you think the receptionist did a good job making the appointment?

Making a Doctor's Appointment

Which Medical Person Should I Contact?

There are many different types of doctors. Read through the list below and choose the right doctor to fit your needs.

- **pediatrician** [piːdiəˈtrɪʃ(ə)n] : works with children and young people
- **surgeon** [sɜː(r)dʒ(ə)n] : performs operations
- **psychiatrist** [saɪˈkaɪətrɪst] : works in mental health
- **anesthesiologist** [ænəsˌθiziˈɑlədʒɪst] : puts people to sleep safely before operations
- **neurologist** [njʊˈrɒlədʒi] : deals in problems involving the brain and nerves
- **oncologist** [ɒnˈkɒlədʒi] : works with people who have cancer
- **rheumatologist** [ruːməˈtɒlədʒi] : deals with joint and limb problems
- **radiologist** [ˌreɪdiˈɒlədʒi] : deals with X-rays, MRI scans, and other tests
- **ophthalmologist** [ɒfθælˈmɒlədʒɪst] : works with people's eyes and vision

4. Language Practice

Using the key words, complete the sentences then practice making your own sentences.

Practice #1 — Suggesting a time

- 4:00 / this afternoon
- tomorrow morning / 9:30 a.m.
- 2:00 p.m. / Wednesday

★ Would _____ at _____ suit you?

★ Could you come in at _____ _____ on _____?

★ How does _____ _____ _____ work for you?

Practice #2 — Making an appointment

- make a doctor's appointment / today
- see the doctor / tomorrow morning
- schedule an appointment / this week

★ Can I _____ sometime later _____?

★ Could I _____ _____?

★ Would it be possible to _____ _____?

Practice #3 — Confirming a time

- How does 5:00 this afternoon work?
- Can you come within the next 30 minutes?
- Do you want to come in tomorrow at 10:00 a.m.?

★ A: _____?
B: Let's make it 10:30 instead.

★ A: _____?
B: Can you squeeze me in a little earlier?

★ A: _____?
B: Pencil me in for 30 minutes from now. I'm on my way.

Lesson 12 / Making a Doctor's Appointment   79

5. Role Plays

Look at the situations and act out the role plays with your partner.

Situation #1

Role A

You are a receptionist at a doctor's office. It is cold season, so the doctor is quite busy. Suggest some possible times for a patient to come in.

1. Answer the phone.
2. Explain that the doctor is extremely busy and the doctor is only available if the patient can come right away.
3. Agree to see the patient if he or she can come right away.

Role B

You woke up sick with the flu. You want to go to the doctor as soon as possible.

1. Explain why you are calling.
2. Try to get an earlier appointment.
3. Promise to leave your house right away.

Situation #2

Role A

You made an appointment for your annual checkup Friday, but you just found out about a last minute business trip. Call to reschedule the appointment. Any weekday morning is good.

1. Tell the receptionist who you are and that you need to reschedule.
2. Ask for an appointment at the beginning of next week.
3. Ask if you can schedule an appointment after the vacation.

Role B

You are a receptionist at a doctor's office. The clinic will be closed next week for vacation. Help a patient schedule an appointment.

1. Confirm the patient's name and the date of the original appointment.
2. Explain your clinic's vacation schedule.
3. Suggest a time and a day for the appointment.

Situational Collocations!

Look at the collocations and try making your own sentences.

helping out	Thank you so much for helping me out.
intensely painful	Kidney and bladder stones can be intensely painful.
splitting headache	I've still got a hangover and a splitting headache.
bad cold	I got soaking wet and caught a bad cold.
minor injury	It's just a minor injury.
deliver a baby	She is due to deliver a baby girl in two weeks.
quick checkup	I think I need to get a quick checkup. I've been having a mild headaches on and off.
diagnosed with cancer	He was diagnosed with stomach cancer, but recovered over the years.

1. ....

2. ....

Making a Doctor's Appointment

Visiting the Dentist!

Dental symptoms related to teeth and gums
- toothache
- pain with chewing
- sensitivity of the teeth
- tooth discoloration
- redness or swelling of the gums
- worn-down teeth
- broken or chipped teeth
- loose or lost teeth

Some factors that cause dental problems
- tooth decay
- infection
- inflammation
- injury
- malnutrition
- certain types of cancer
- inherited disorders

Names of our teeth

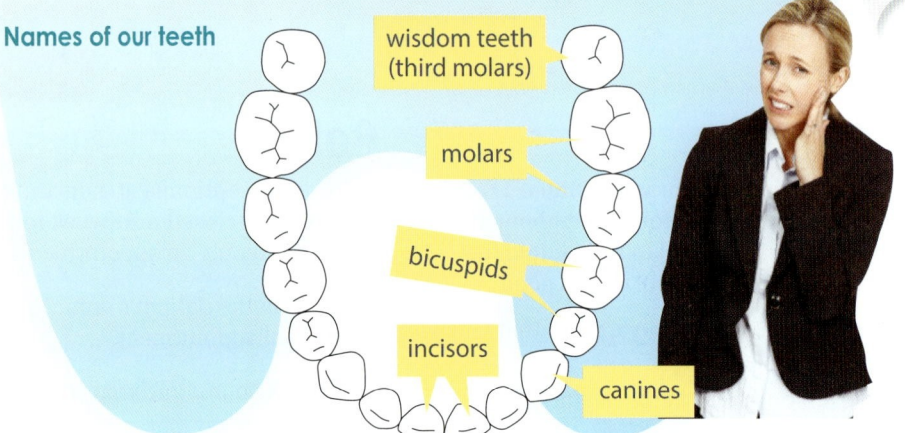

- wisdom teeth (third molars)
- molars
- bicuspids
- incisors
- canines

"Good morning, Dr. David's office. How may I help you?"

"Hi, this is Kelly Clark. I'd like to make an appointment."

"Could you explain the symptoms a little?"

"I have … _____"

6. Cultural Discussion Questions

Talk about the questions in as much detail as possible.

1. Do people in your country usually have regular family doctors, or do they go directly to specialists when they need them?

2. In your country, is it common to take time off work to go to the doctor?

3. Do you prefer traditional medicine or Western medicine? Explain.

4. Are all medical bills covered by insurance in your country, or do you have to pay extra for some clinics and services?

Did You Know?

Read and discuss how you feel about each fact.

1. Did you know that in the US, the average *doctor's appointment* only lasts for **18 minutes** or less?

2. Did you know that **health spending** per person in the U.S. was **$10,348** in **2016**? That is **31% higher** than **Switzerland**, the second highest spender.

Medical Tourism

1. Most people who travel for medical care are seeking better care or lower costs. The reasons cited by nearly 50,000 patients worldwide who sought foreign care are listed below:

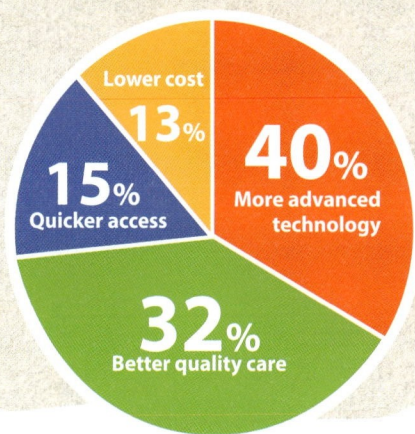

2. One of the most famous destinations for medical tourism is India. Many people say some advantages for medical tourists in India are:

- Low cost
- Less waiting time
- The availability of the latest medical technology
- A growing compliance with international quality standards
- Less likely to face a language barrier

Q. Have you ever considered medical tourism for yourself?

7. Slang & Idioms

Match the slang phrases and idioms with their definitions and use them to complete the sentences below.

1. ___ walk-in clinic
2. ___ call in a prescription
3. ___ over-the-counter
4. ___ moment to spare
5. ___ flu shot

A. sold by ordinary retail purchase, with no need for a prescription
B. free time
C. a medical facility that accepts patients without an appointment
D. when a doctor's office contacts a pharmacy to fill a prescription without visiting the doctor
E. a vaccine to prevent a strain of influenza

1. When I have a cold, all I usually need is some _____ medication.
2. Every year, I make sure to get a _____, so I won't get sick.
3. If you can't get a doctor's appointment, you can always try over at the _____.
4. The doctor doesn't have a _____ in his schedule today.
5. I needed a refill of my allergy medication, so I had the doctor _____.

Wrapping Up!

Write down four things you learned from this lesson and review.

1
2
3
4

New Get Up To Speed+ Book 2
SLANG & IDIOM GLOSSARY

Lesson 1

average Joe	a completely average person
dead ringer	a person that looks exactly like someone else
easy on the eyes	classically handsome or pretty
picture-perfect	lacking in defects or flaws
salt and pepper hair	a blend of a person's natural hair color along with gray

Lesson 2

get away from it all	to escape from everyday life
hit the trail	to begin a journey
run out of gas	to run out of energy
set up camp	to prepare an area for sleeping outside
weather / cooperate with us	for weather will be like one hopes for

Lesson 3

a steal	a bargain
BOGO	buy one, get one free
dry clean only	to clean with chemicals that have little or no water
fast fashion	an approach to the production of clothing that makes trends quickly and cheaply available in stores
slashed its prices	to greatly reduce the cost of an item

Lesson 4

call ahead	to call in advance
on an empty stomach	without eating anything
order in	to order delivery food from a restaurant
wined and dined	to try to impress someone with an expensive meal
you are what you eat	eat good food in order to be healthy

Lesson 5

head honcho	the highest ranking person
making bank	to earn a large amount of money
on top of the world	happy and elated
This calls for a celebration!	We should celebrate!
word on the street	a rumor or piece of information currently being circulated

Lesson 6

burn off	to get rid of energy or fat through exercise
drop a few pounds	to lose weight
get in a workout	to fit exercise in a tight schedule
spare tire	a roll of fat around a person's waist
swim some laps	to swim the length of a pool repeatedly

Lesson 7

asking price	the price at which something is offered for sale
counteroffer	an offer made in response to another
fixer-upper	a house in need of repairs
have a roof over our heads	have a place to live
throwing money down the drain	wasting money

Lesson 8

wasn't a seat in the house	no available seats
booked solid	to be fully reserved
last resort	a final course of action, used only when all else has failed
no show	a person who makes a reservation but fails to come or cancel it
waiting list	a list of people waiting for something

Lesson 9

a toss-up	a situation in which all outcomes or options are equally possible
down to the wire	a situation whose outcome is not decided until the very last minute
neck and neck	even in a race or competition
on the edge of my seat	very excited and giving one's full attention to something
throw in the towel	to give up

Lesson 10

bounced	a transaction cannot be processed because of nonsufficient funds
direct debit	a payment system where creditors are authorized to charge a customer's bank account directly
froze my account	an action taken by a bank that prevents any transactions from occurring
in the red	to have spent more money than one has in an account
nest egg	a sum of money saved for the future

Lesson 11

advance warning	notice beforehand
ditch	to get rid of
double-booked	to accidentally make appointments at a conflicting time
flake	an unreliable person
leave me hanging	to keep someone waiting for your decision or answer

Lesson 12

call in a prescription	when a doctor's office contacts a pharmacy to fill a prescription without visiting the doctor
flu shot	a vaccine to prevent a strain of influenza
moment to spare	free time
over-the-counter	sold by ordinary retail purchase, with no need for a prescription
walk-in clinic	a medical facility that accepts patients without an appointment

New Get Up To Speed+ Book 2
ANSWER KEY

Lesson 1

Useful Expressions

a   2
b   3
c   4
d   1

Language Practice

Practice #1
★   all
★   all
★   all

Practice #2
★   chubby
★   180cm
★   chubby or petite

Practice #3
★   How tall / What height
★   What color
★   hairstyle

Slang & Idioms

1   C   easy on the eyes
2   E   salt and pepper hair
3   A   average Joe
4   B   picture-perfect
5   D   dead ringer

Lesson 2

Useful Expressions

a   4
b   3
c   2
d   1

Language Practice

Practice #1
★   skiing
★   gardening
★   hiking

Practice #2
★   kayak / the Amazon River
★   climb / Mt. Everest
★   go snorkeling / the Great Barrier Reef

Practice #3
★   for a run / snow or hiking / rain
★   skiing / warm
★   for a run / snow or hiking / rain

Slang & Idioms

1   D   get away from it all
2   C   weather / cooperate with us
3   E   set up camp
4   A   hit the trail
5   B   run out of gas

Lesson 3

Useful Expressions

a   4
b   3
c   1
d   2

Language Practice

Practice #1
★   on sale or on clearance
★   all
★   on sale or on clearance

Practice #2
★   other lengths
★   another size
★   different color

Practice #3
★ make me look fat or look too long
★ flattering
★ make me look fat or look too long

Slang & Idioms

1	E	a steal
2	C	slashed its prices
3	A	BOGO
4	B	fast fashion
5	D	dry clean only

Lesson 4

Useful Expressions

a	4
b	2
c	1
d	3

Language Practice

Practice #1
★ all
★ all
★ all

Practice #2
★ grabbing a drink
★ catch up over dinner
★ hit up

Practice #3
★ try anything once
★ in the mood for
★ to die for

Slang & Idioms

1	C	on an empty stomach
2	B	wined and dined
3	A	you are what you eat
4	E	call ahead

5   D   order in

Lesson 5

Useful Expressions

a	3
b	4
c	2
d	1

Language Practice

Practice #1
★ all
★ all
★ all

Practice #2
★ promotion / CEO or promotion / Division Head
★ transferred / overseas
★ promotion / CEO or promotion / Division Head

Practice #3
★ all
★ all
★ all

Slang & Idioms

1	B	word on the street
2	D	head honcho
3	A	on top of the world
4	E	making bank
5	C	This calls for a celebration

Lesson 6

Useful Expressions

a	3
b	4
c	1
d	2

New Get Up To Speed+ Book 2
ANSWER KEY

Language Practice

Practice #1
- all
- all
- all

Practice #2
- run on the treadmill
- stretching
- do strength training

Practice #3
- exercise before work
- lifting weights
- going to the gym

Slang & Idioms

1	E	drop a few pounds
2	C	spare tire
3	A	burn off
4	B	get in a workout
5	D	swim some laps

Lesson 7

Useful Expressions

a	3
b	4
c	2
d	1

Language Practice

Practice #1
- dimensions
- floor plan
- square footage

Practice #2
- kitchen / appliances
- house / security system
- walk-in closet / master

Practice #3
- counteroffer / small changes
- put down / $20,000
- put in an offer / $170,000

Slang & Idioms

1	C	counteroffer
2	A	asking price
3	B	fixer-upper
4	D	have a roof over our heads
5	E	throwing money

Lesson 8

Useful Expressions

a	3
b	2
c	4
d	1

Language Practice

Practice #1
- private rooms
- tables / 7:00 p.m.
- tomorrow night

Practice #2
- fully booked
- make a reservation or reserve a table
- make a reservation or reserve a table

Practice #3
- party platters or booster seats
- booth
- party platters or booster seats

Slang & Idioms

1	D	waiting list
2	B	wasn't a seat in the house
3	A	no show
4	E	last resort

5	C	booked solid

Lesson 9

Useful Expressions

a	1
b	3
c	4
d	2

Language Practice

Practice #1
★ ended in triumph
★ got slaughtered
★ came in second

Practice #2
★ take it all or go all the way
★ picking / to win
★ take it all or go all the way

Practice #3
★ tough call
★ tight game
★ well-matched

Slang & Idioms

1	D	neck and neck
2	E	down to the wire
3	B	a toss-up
4	C	on the edge of my seat
5	A	throw in the towel

Lesson 10

Useful Expressions

a	4
b	1
c	2
d	3

Language Practice

Practice #1
★ withdraw / $350
★ open / savings account
★ deposit / checking account

Practice #2
★ all
★ all
★ savings account

Practice #3
★ bank statement
★ photo ID or ATM card
★ photo ID or ATM card

Slang & Idioms

1	C	in the red
2	E	direct debit
3	B	froze my account
4	A	bounced
5	D	nest egg

Lesson 11

Useful Expressions

a	2
b	1
c	3
d	4

Language Practice

Practice #1
★ feeling up to it
★ something going on
★ made other plans

Practice #2
★ not into that
★ something else
★ some other time

New Get Up To Speed+ Book 2
ANSWER KEY

Practice #3
- I'm sorry, but I can't make it on Friday.
- I have other plans that night.
- Sorry, but can I take a rain check?

Slang & Idioms
1	E	advance warning
2	C	ditch
3	A	flake
4	B	double-booked
5	D	leave me hanging

Slang & Idioms
1	C	over-the-counter
2	D	flu shot
3	A	walk-in clinic
4	B	moment to spare
5	E	call in a prescription

Lesson 12

Useful Expressions
a	4
b	1
c	2
d	3

Language Practice

Practice #1
- tomorrow morning / 9:30 a.m.
- 2:00 p.m. / Wednesday
- 4:00 / this afternoon

Practice #2
- all
- all
- all

Practice #3
- How does 5:00 this afternoon work? or Do you want to come in tomorrow at 10:00 a.m.?
- How does 5:00 this afternoon work? or Do you want to come in tomorrow at 10:00 a.m.?
- Can you come within the next 30 minutes?